# THE KITCHEN GOD'S WIFE

## NOTES

*ncluding*

- *Life and Background*
- *Introduction to the Novel*
- *A Brief Synopsis*
- *List of Characters*
- *Chronology of Historical and Fictional Events*
- *Critical Commentaries*
- *Genealogies*
- *Map*
- *Critical Essays*
    - Character Analysis: Winnie Louie
    - Tan's Literary Ingredients
    - Settings
    - The Asian-American Literary Phenomenon
- *Review Questions and Essay Topics*
- *Amy Tan's Published Works*
- *Selected Bibliography*
- *Historical Background Bibliography*

*by*
*Mei Li Robinson*
*University of North Carolina at Greensboro*

INCORPORATED

LINCOLN, NEBRASKA 68501

| Editor | Consulting Editor |
|---|---|
| *Gary Carey, M.A.* <br> *University of Colorado* | *James L. Roberts, Ph.D.* <br> *Department of English* <br> *University of Nebraska* |

ISBN 0-8220-0712-6
© Copyright 1996
by
**Cliffs Notes, Inc.**
All Rights Reserved
Printed in U.S.A.

1996 Printing

Cliffs Notes, Inc.          Lincoln, Nebraska

# CONTENTS

# THE KITCHEN GOD'S WIFE

## Notes

### LIFE AND BACKGROUND

Amy Tan—one of American literature's freshest, most energetic Asian-American superstars—has successfully allied herself with two driving forces in the book market of the late twentieth century: **feminism** and **cross-culturalism**. This favorable union of themes and style, however, doesn't spring from a calculated attempt to manipulate the fiction market, but from Tan's internal wars with society, self, mother, and the past.

Tan herself resembles the first-generation Chinese-American characters who people her bestselling **inter-generational** tapestries, *The Joy Luck Club* (1989), *The Kitchen God's Wife* (1991), and *The Hundred Secret Senses* (1995). Inspired by the stories of memorable women throughout her mother's life, Tan has in these books honored a sisterhood whose power and vitality are as influential to her writing as is her unique cultural background.

**Early Years.** Born An-Mei Tan on February 19, 1952, in Oakland, California, Amy Tan was the second of three children and the only daughter of John Tan and Daisy Tu Ching Tan. John was a Beijing-born electrical engineer and volunteer Baptist minister, and Daisy was an industrial nurse and medical technician from Shanghai. The Tans had immigrated to California in the late 1940s, when post-war China was remolding its society to fit its concept of communism.

Coming of age in a predominantly Caucasian society in a succession of California cities—Fresno, Berkeley, San Francisco, and Santa Clara—Amy Tan gave little thought to her Chinese relatives or to her mother's first marriage prior to her emigration from China.

Because she was brought up as an American, she felt disconnected from her Asian-American heritage for which her mother was both spokesperson and role model. In fact, Amy resented her parents earmarking their savings for needy Chinese relatives.

Amy challenged parental authority, yet met John and Daisy Tan's expectations of high achievement by studying piano and excelling in science and math. Amy's emotional rootlessness led her to distance herself from Daisy, who chose Amy's careers—concert pianist and physician—instead of a vocation in one of the less remunerative liberal arts.

Family relationships were severely strained by two agonizingly slow deaths—in 1967, Amy's seventeen-year-old brother, Peter, and in 1968, her fifty-four-year-old father, John—both victims of brain tumors. Amy's normal adolescent stresses, heightened by intense grief, pushed her into serious rebellion. Daisy Tan felt it necessary to leave California, so the family moved to Montreux, Switzerland, where Amy and her younger brother John were enrolled in a private school. Despite the foreign setting, Amy's rebelliousness flared up and she enjoyed a brief flirtation with a German involved in crime and drugs before her mother helped the police take him into custody in a risky trap at the border.

**College Education.**   When the family returned to San Francisco, Amy's scholarships and part-time work at a pizzeria paid her tuition at Linfield, a small Baptist college in McMinnville, Oregon. She pursued a medical degree on her way to a career in neurosurgery, a choice that met Daisy's standards.

Amy's need to rebel and to shock her mother lessened after she gave up scruffy overalls, stopped dating hippies, and settled on Lou DeMattei, a pre-law student and likely husband material. The romance flourished during six months of silence between mother and daughter. Then, transferring in her sophomore year to San Jose State University to be with Lou, Amy encountered a new adversary—a disapproving future mother-in-law. This relationship required the intervention of Daisy, a tenacious, eighty-pound scrapper, who defended her daughter and won.

No longer certain she wanted to be a doctor, Amy switched majors and received a degree in English in 1973, followed by an M.A. in linguistics from San Jose State and groundwork for a doctorate at the University of California at Berkeley. In 1974, she left graduate school, married Lou, a tax attorney, and settled in a San Francisco condominium.

Four years later, after Daisy returned from a trip to China, Amy and her mother patched up their differences as adults—woman to woman—having survived the worst of their alienation. For the first time, Amy Tan could acknowledge the double strands of Chinese and American traditions embellishing her past.

**Writing.** As an employee of the Alameda County Association for Retarded Citizens, Amy worked as a language consultant to the mentally handicapped before becoming a journalist in 1979. For three years, she wrote and edited news, and then launched and helped publish a professional journal, *Emergency Room Reports*.

During this period, her mother divulged the hard facts of her previous marriage in China, of a son who died in infancy, and of three daughters she had left behind and never mentioned to her American children. Amy began a sisterly correspondence. In 1991, she helped one sister, a nurse, emigrate from China to Wisconsin with her surgeon husband and their fourteen-year-old daughter; the couple found work managing a Chinese restaurant. In *The Hundred Secret Senses*, Tan includes as one of the main characters a half-sister born in China and brought to the U.S. to be part of her father's second family.

In "Watching China," a 1989 article in *Glamour*, Tan reported the violent backlash against striking freedom fighters in Tiananmen Square, where Chinese students risked death in their push for democracy. Closer to home, Tan faced an insidious threat to her well-being. Overwork and inner discontent preceded three stressful events: Daisy's hospitalization for an acute attack of angina, Amy's own unsuccessful psychiatric therapy, and her third career change. She now freelanced a diverse and demanding load of technical writing, including speeches and monographs, and provided a telephone astrology service, which consumed ninety hours a week, providing enough money from fees to pay for Daisy's new home. Amy tried relaxing with sessions of jazz piano, evenings of billiards with Lou, and books by notable female writers—Eudora Welty, Flannery O'Connor, Isabel Allende, Kay Gibbons, and Louise Erdrich. Yet she needed a more substantial safety valve than piano keys, pool cues, and books to relieve mounting pressures.

She began penning flimsy, imitative works based on popular

fiction; the stories received a steady response of rejection notices. At the Squaw Valley Community of Writers workshop, she came under the influence of award-winning writer and feminist mentor Molly Giles. With further encouragement from agent Sandra Dijkstra, Tan began writing articles and short fiction for *Atlantic Monthly, FM, Glamour, Grazia, Ladies' Home Journal, Life, McCall's, Publishers Weekly, Threepenny Review, San Francisco Focus, Seventeen,* and *Short Story Review.* She also worked on novels, including historical fiction, and polished "Endgame," the complex short story begun at Squaw Valley that later formed a **pivotal episode** in *The Joy Luck Club,* a **blended narrative** about four Chinese-American women and their mothers.

A skilled **raconteur** capable of juggling wit, insight, and pathos within a single unified scene, Tan excels in **oral tradition** and complex emotional involvements. These skills, as first reflected in *The Joy Luck Club,* earned her a Commonwealth Club gold award, the Bay Area Book Reviewers award for best fiction, an American Library Association citation for best book for young adults, and nominations for the National Book Critics Circle's best novel and for the *Los Angeles Times'* best book of 1989. Tan sold the paperback rights to *The Joy Luck Club* to G. P. Putnam's Ivy Books for $1.23 million, and the work has since been translated and distributed in seventeen languages. In 1993, Wayne Wang directed the Disney studio's screen version, which was co-produced by Oliver Stone and co-scripted by Amy Tan and Ron Bass, Oscar-winning author of *Rain Man.*

After *The Kitchen God's Wife* was successful, Tan began writing more to please herself than for the fickle critics and media who seemed intent on defining her as a feminist/Asian-American/memoirist. She teamed with illustrator Gretchen Schields to create *The Moon Lady,* a children's legend extracted from the misadventures of Ying-ying in *The Joy Luck Club.* Focused on wish-fulfillment through personal action rather than through divine intervention and graced with Manchu-style drawings, the story is a visual and textual success. More recently, the two collaborated again on another children's book, *The Chinese Siamese Cat* (1994).

Turning from female **protagonists** extrapolated from her mother's side of the family, Tan began work on *The Year of No Flood* in which the main character is a young boy. This historical novel about mission work—her father's calling—is set during the nineteenth century's Boxer Rebellion. She eventually set that work aside to complete her third published novel, *The Hundred Secret Senses* (1995), which debuted in sixth place on the bestseller list. It continues to draw upon her unique experiences with family relationships as well as upon her cultural heritage, especially the traditions of Chinese spirits and ghosts.

As a multiple dropout—from medical training, from her profession of speech pathology, from journalism, and from psychotherapy—Amy Tan finds greater solace and inner worth through composing family-based fiction and nonfiction. Although she achieved stardom in both feminist and multicultural literary circles in a remarkable three-year period, she shuns arbitrary categorization and keeps her options open. No longer denying her cultural roots on either side of the family, Amy Tan is remarkably at home with things Chinese, which serve as the counterpoint to her American independence and entrepreneurial spirit.

## INTRODUCTION TO THE NOVEL

Since Tan realized such phenomenal success with her first published book, *The Joy Luck Club*, a reader might assume she could immediately go on to write another blockbuster novel. Our literature, however, abounds with memorable first novels by authors who never published another successful book. Appreciation of *The Kitchen God's Wife* can be enhanced by learning how Tan carried out the awesome task of its creation.

Tan admits to feeling daunted by the success of *The Joy Luck Club* as she approached the writing of her next book. She shuffled through six plots and wearying weeks of book tours, speeches, volunteer projects, and literary luncheons. Finally, she settled in with incense and recorded music over earphones—plus a telephone-answering machine to assure herself of the privacy and calm she needed. In "Angst and the Second Novel," a 1991 essay for *Publishers Weekly*, she confided that writing demands "persistence imposed by a limited focus." To that end, she fenced herself in as if she were "a priest, a nun, a convict serving a life's sentence."

Despite her concentration, self-doubts led her through a nightmarish procession of characters, plots, and discarded false starts—a tale about a girl orphaned in the San Francisco earthquake of 1906, one set in Mongolia as described in the Manchu language, another about a potent elixir that accidentally poisons a magistrate, and yet another about the daughter of a missionary to China in the 1930s.

In "Lost Lives of Women," a *Life* magazine essay, Tan divulges a maternal background with obvious parallels to this novel's plot. Daisy Tan's mother, Jingmei, came from a refined background and married a poor scholar who died from influenza before he could assume a worthy job in a magistrate's office. Unprotected as a widow in a fiercely patriarchal society, Jingmei was raped and forced to join the rapist's household as a concubine shrouded in shame and dishonor.

To preserve her son's dignity, Jingmei abandoned him and immigrated with nine-year-old Daisy (called "Baobei," or Treasure) to an island off the Shanghai coast. After giving birth to a second son, Jingmei killed herself by concealing a lethal dose of opium in a New Year's rice cake. Daisy related Jingmei's story to Amy to illustrate the powerlessness of women in China in the 1920s.

Tan developed a talkative woman character, but lost her focus until it occurred to her to make the story a gift—from herself as speaker to listener Daisy, who inspired the exchange after wondering aloud what her daughter would remember about her. In the reflective interview for *Publishers Weekly*, she claims:

> I had to fight for every single character, every image, every word. And the story is, in fact, about a woman who does the same thing: she fights to believe in herself. . . . She is no innocent. She sees her fears, but she no longer lets them chase her.

Daisy has equated Amy's muse with the ghost of Jingmei, Amy's much maligned, but indomitable grandmother. When Amy and her mother visited Daisy's brother (the son that Jingmei had abandoned in Shanghai) in Beijing, China, Tan and her uncle agreed that Jingmei "is the source of strength running through our family." This verbal tribute moved Daisy to tears, releasing anxieties and sorrows of her early life.

In a **sidebar** accompanying an excerpt from *The Kitchen God's Wife*, published in *McCall's*, Tan says that the transfer of hope from mother to daughter is the key to the story. The novel satisfied Tan's expectations to "write something deeper and wider [than *The Joy Luck Club*] . . . something that examines many of the toughest issues in my life"—and of her mother's life. The book is Tan's effort to dispel the ghosts of her mother's wretched marriage and her experiences in China during the war with Japan. Tan dedicated the book "to my mother, Daisy Tan, and her happy memories of my father, John . . . and my brother Peter . . . with love and respect."

In its paralleling of real and fictional elements, the book resembles a **roman á clef**, a shadow saga of the Tan family:

- the resemblance of fictional heroine Winnie Louie to real-life Daisy Tan and the resemblance of the malignant Wen Fu to Jingmei's unnamed rapist-husband
- the dual tragedies of Daisy's and Winnie's mothers, whose hopes are destroyed by men who devalue them, treating them not as human beings, but as pleasure-giving possessions
- the social mores of a patriarchal society that spawn feudal marriages intended to enrich or ennoble the groom and his family
- the chaotic wartime circumstances that force change on an outmoded government as well as on its citizens
- the settlement of the Tan family and of Winnie and Jimmy Louie in California before the Communists halt emigration from China
- the reunion of Chinese family members with Asian-American relatives who dimly appreciate their relatives' struggles
- the revelation of early episodes that shed light both on past hurts and debilitating regrets and on the disunity and misunderstandings that flourish in the present.

On one hand, *The Kitchen God's Wife* echoes the oral foundation, the confessional style, the theme of alienation, sweeping war scenarios, and mother-daughter situations of *The Joy Luck Club*. On the other hand, it has merited comparison to the darkly dramatic novels of Russian literary giants Leo Tolstoy, Feodor Dostoevsky, and Boris Pasternak.

The strength of *The Kitchen God's Wife* and its predecessor is Tan's skill at delineating wisps of love and admiration in the ragged, indirect, yet hurtful set-tos and silences between mother and daughter and at revealing the family secrets that chew like canker worms into the most vulnerable recesses of the family's heart.

The completed book sold quickly to Putnam, the publisher of

her first book. The Literary Guild purchased distribution rights fo
$425,000, and pre-publication sales were made to five foreign pub
lishers. Neither her readers nor her publisher have been disap
pointed: *The Kitchen God's Wife* held its place on *Publishers Weekly*
list of hardcover bestsellers for thirty-eight weeks. By the spring o
1991, *The Kitchen God's Wife* topped a quarter million sales as :
headed into paperback for even wider distribution. It was nom
nated for a Bay Area Book Reviewers award and was selected a
1991 editor's choice by *Booklist*.

The financial as well as the critical success of *The Kitchen God'*
*Wife* squelched fears that Amy Tan had already published her bes
work with *The Joy Luck Club*.

## A BRIEF SYNOPSIS

Opening in San Francisco in January 1990, an extended Ch
nese-American family gathers for a dual purpose—an engagemer
dinner and a funeral. The first narrator, Pearl Louie Brandt, cor
ceals a seven-year struggle with multiple sclerosis from her wid
owed mother, Winnie. At the banquet, Pearl learns that Heler
Winnie's best friend and co-owner of a flower shop, knows abou
the disease and threatens to pass the news to Winnie as part of th
Chinese New Year ritual of clearing the air of secrets. Pearl accep*
the fact that she herself must tell her mother about the disease.

The Buddhist funeral of Helen's Auntie Du releases in Pea
the grief she has repressed for her father, Jimmy Louie, a Bapti
minister, who died a quarter century earlier, when Pearl was fou
teen. From Auntie Du, Pearl inherits a table altar to the Kitche
God, a deceitful husband and a judge of who gets good luck an
who gets bad.

After the banquet and funeral, Helen shares with Winnie
letter informing her that Wen Fu, Winnie's former abusive husban
has died of heart disease. Just as Helen has threatened to tell Pearl
secret to Winnie before the New Year, Helen now threatens Winn
that she will tell Pearl about Winnie's secret-filled life, now that We
Fu is dead—unless Winnie tells Pearl about it herself.

That story, told by Winnie to Pearl, is the novel's major focus,
long and intense narrative, structured by many episodes:

- Winnie's early life as Jiang Weili, daughter of Jiang Sao-yen, a Shanghai textile factory owner
- her abandonment at the age of six by her vain mother and subsequently by her father
- her early marriage to—and humiliation by—the selfish, abusive Wen Fu, a pilot for China's new air force
- her long and stormy friendship with Hulan, wife of Wen Fu's boss
- the individual and cooperative struggles to survive the invasion of China by the Japanese
- the births and deaths of three children
- the continued and escalating abuse by Wen Fu
- Winnie's encounters with Jimmy Louie, first at an American dance and much later on a Shanghai street
- her arrest, trial, and imprisonment
- her flight from Wen Fu and China to Jimmy Louie and California in 1949; and finally,
- the reunion with Hulan, now Helen, and the resumption of their quarrelsome friendship (Winnie claimed that Helen was her sister by marriage so that Helen and her family could emigrate from Formosa to the U.S.).

The gnawing ache in Winnie's relationship with Pearl springs from continual fear about Wen Fu, whom she suspects is Pearl's father. Recalling the perverted joy Wen Fu took in abusing them all, Winnie still grieves for Mochou, her stillborn first daughter; for Yiku, her second daughter, who died after Wen Fu's cruelty and neglect; and for Danru, who died far from his mother while she was attempting to divorce Wen Fu. Later, she sees in Pearl a likeness to all three of these children.

With gold given to her secretly by her mute, ailing father and with encouragement from a rebellious cousin and from Jimmy Louie, Weili (Winnie) makes plans to flee not only her marriage, but also Shanghai and China. Wen Fu foils the plot and has Weili arrested. At her trial, Weili elects to spend two years in prison rather than return to her impossible marriage. In the scandal stimulated by the trial, Jimmy Louie loses his job as interpreter and must return to the United States. He vows to return in two years and meanwhile he supports her with letters and gifts of American dollars.

Auntie Du obtains Weili's early release from prison in the spring of 1949 by intimidating corrupt officials. Through trickery, Weili forces Wen Fu to sign divorce papers; Wen Fu avenges himself by stalking her, ripping up the divorce papers, threatening to steal the plane tickets, and raping Weili at gunpoint. She captures his gun and forces him trouserless into the street. She leaves China by plane the next day, narrowly escaping occupation of Shanghai by the Communists, who ban all emigration. She settles with Jimmy in California, fearful that the child she bears may be the offspring of Wen Fu, inheriting his evil traits.

When Winnie concludes her life story, Pearl ends a quarter-century of mother-daughter alienation by disclosing her multiple sclerosis to her mother. Plans form for a trip to China to seek herbal treatments and cures.

To seal their new-found comfort with the truth, Winnie burns the picture of the cruel Kitchen God and selects for Pearl a new icon for the red temple altar: Lady Sorrowfree.

# LIST OF CHARACTERS

## WINNIE'S ORIGINAL FAMILY (SHANGHAI)

### Jiang Weili (Winnie Louie, Weiwei, Ha-bu)

Jiang Weili was born in 1918 into a wealthy home in Shanghai, China. As the novel begins in 1990, Weili uses the nickname "Winnie" given to her by her late American husband, Jimmy Louie. Her narration of her "secret" life story to her daughter Pearl forms the core of the novel. Through the challenges of her life in wartime China, she replaces insecurity, dependence, and self-deprecation with peace of mind, self-assurance, and independence. Her granddaughters lovingly call her "Ha-bu."

### Jiang Sao-yen

Weili's father, a dignified, successful Shanghai businessman, owns the Five Phoenixes Textile Factories and grows wealthy enough through his exports to marry several wives and to give his younger, less able brother a factory and the largest house on Tsungming Island.

## Weili's Mother

Never named in the novel, she is the beautiful and vain second-ranking wife of Jiang Sao-yen. Being the second "second wife" (the other, a suicide), she is dubbed his "double second." A modern, educated woman with unbound feet and a taste for foreign luxuries, she disappears when Weili is six, leaving Weili to the care of her father and his other wives, who soon send her to her uncle's family.

## San Ma

Jiang's third wife, she plays a significant background role at several crisis points in the novel: she probably helps Jiang decide to send Weili to Tsungming Island to live; she helps Weili select her trousseau; she takes care of Jiang after his disability; she tells Weili what happened during the war; she supports Weili's departure; and, with Wu Ma, she tells Weili about her father's death. Weili recognizes her qualities when she says to San Ma, "What a good person you are."

# WINNIE'S FOSTER FAMILY (TSUNGMING ISLAND)

## Uncle

Jiang Sao-yen's younger brother, he lives in the largest house on Tsungming Island and manages a factory given to him by Jiang. He and his wives give Weili a home from 1925 to 1937 while she attends a Catholic boarding school in Shanghai.

## Old Aunt

Jiang's brother's first wife, she is rigid about rules for proper behavior. In later years it is clear Old Aunt loves Weili, has a natural sense of humor, and feels shame about their circumstances after the war.

## New Aunt

The second wife of Jiang's younger brother and mother of Peanut, Little Gong, and Little Gao—all cousins of Weili. New Aunt and Weili's mother had been classmates at the missionary school in Shanghai.

### Jiang Huazheng ("Peanut")

Huazheng, Weili's cousin, daughter of Uncle and New Aunt, is called Peanut (Huasheng in Chinese) "because she was small and plump like the two rounds of a peanut shell." Because she tries to be worldly, modern, and even shocking, she serves as a **foil** to the naive young Weili. Ironically, unable to marry Wen Fu, she marries into a relationship that is even more untenable than had she married Wen Fu; her marriage is so unbearable, in fact, that it leads to her divorce and isolation from her mother and father.

### Little Gong and Little Gao

Weili's boy cousins, sons of Uncle and New Aunt; Peanut's younger brothers.

## WINNIE'S FIRST MARRIAGE AND FAMILY (CHINA)

### Wen Fu

Weili's abusive first husband and her primary source of suffering throughout much of her young life, he is a scheming opportunist and incorrigible womanizer; he tries to control everyone around him and runs roughshod over anyone who gets in his way.

### Mochou

A girl, the stillborn first child of Weili and Wen Fu; her name means "sorrowfree."

### Yiku

The second daughter of Weili and Wen Fu; her name means "sorrow over bitterness." She dies of a severe illness before reaching her first birthday.

### Danru

Weili and Wen Fu's third child and first son, his name means "nonchalance." When he is about seven, Weili flees with him from Wen Fu to Jimmy Louie. They eventually must send him away from Shanghai, and he dies in an epidemic far from his mother.

## WINNIE'S SECOND MARRIAGE
## AND FAMILY (CALIFORNIA)

### James Y. Louie (Jimmy)

This gentle, winsome Chinese-American is a translator for the U. S. Information Service. He meets and flirts with Weili at a Christmas dance sponsored by the Americans in Kunming in 1941, and he gives her an American nickname, Winnie. Five years later, they meet accidentally in Shanghai and become friends and lovers. Three years later, Weili flees to America to marry Jimmy, who has become a Christian minister.

### Pearl Louie Brandt

Winnie's daughter. Born after Winnie's arrival in the U.S. and marriage to Jimmy Louie, she is the wife of Phil Brandt and the mother of young Tessa and Cleo and works as a speech therapist for children with disabilities. Pearl has been diagnosed with multiple sclerosis.

### Samuel Louie

Winnie's son, born in 1952, he lives in New Jersey in 1990.

### Phil Brandt

Pearl's Caucasian husband and San Jose pathologist, he tries to protect Pearl from a full-fledged attack of multiple sclerosis and seems frustrated that he can't do more.

### Tessa and Cleo

Pearl and Phil's daughters (ages eight and three respectively in 1990).

## HELEN KWONG'S FAMILIES
## (CHINA AND CALIFORNIA)

### Hulan (Helen Kwong)

A poorly educated woman from outside Loyang, she is first married to Long Jiaguo, a pilot and a superior officer of Wen Fu. Weili meets Hulan shortly after marrying Wen Fu, when he reports to Hangchow for pilot training. Hulan becomes Weili's lifelong friend in an outspoken relationship that seems to flourish on their differences. She also becomes Winnie's partner in a flower shop in San Francisco. Initially, Pearl thinks that Helen is her aunt.

### Long Jiaguo

A vice-captain in China's new air force, he is head of the second trained air squadron that includes Wen Fu, Gan, and other new pilots. A temperate, reasonable man and effective officer, eventually promoted to captain, he is Hulan's husband when she meets Weili.

### Auntie Du Ching

Hulan's aggressive, superstitious, opinionated, and kindly aunt, she is the widow of Helen's paternal uncle, and mother of a daughter who joins the Communists. A courageous refugee from Peking, Auntie Du saves her money and flees the Japanese to join Hulan in Kunming. After her immigration to the U.S., Winnie watches out for Auntie Du's welfare until her death at age ninety-seven in 1990.

### Henry Kwong (Kuang An)

Helen's second husband; his Chinese name is Kuang An.

### Roger Kwong

Helen and Henry Kwong's son, he is nicknamed Bao-bao. Twice married and divorced and recently rid of an engagement, he is again becoming engaged, this time to Mimi Wong, the celebration of which is one reason for the family gathering at the novel's opening.

### Mary Kwong Cheu

The daughter of Helen and Henry Kwong, she is the mother of Michael and Jennifer. Mary lives in Los Angeles and is married to Doug Cheu. Mary and Doug introduced Pearl to Phil Brandt and know about Pearl's multiple sclerosis.

### Frank Kwong

The second son of Helen and Henry Kwong.

## OTHER CHARACTERS

### Lin

Weili's first suitor, whom she rejects at age sixteen, and whom she meets again when he is a successful doctor in Fresno.

### Gan

*Dies*

A mild-mannered, gentlemanly pilot in Jiaguo's squadron, he admires Weili's cooking, confides in her, spends time with her.

### Wan Betty

*B+*

A chance acquaintance who works as a telegraph operator in Nanking and later in Shanghai, she writes a letter to Helen about Wen Fu's death.

### Min

*Dies*

She is a stage-struck, illiterate concubine whom Wen Fu installs in his home while Weili gives birth to Danru; Weili befriends and helps her.

### Little Yu's Mother

She is a widow whose daughter has hanged herself rather than endure an impossible marriage. With Peanut's help, she assists in the management of the Shanghai waystation for runaway wives.

### Old Mr. Ma

He is the skilled and crusty old driver of the truck with nine passengers, including Weili, fleeing from Nanking over fourteen hundred miles to Kunming.

### Auntie Miao

An elderly matchmaker on Tsungming Island, she introduces Wen Fu's parents to New Aunt and Peanut, and indirectly to Weili.

### Mimi Wong

Roger Kwong's young third wife.

# CHRONOLOGY OF HISTORICAL
# AND FICTIONAL EVENTS

Throughout *The Kitchen God's Wife*, Tan interweaves critical events of Chinese history with the fictional experiences of her characters. The historical events are not simply employed to provide color and realism, but are integral influences on the story itself. The chronology outlined below includes several historical events which are not mentioned in the novel, but which play a significant role in the novel's historical and fictional events—for example, the U.S. entry into World War II and the U.S. bombing of Hiroshima.

| DATE | FACT | FICTION |
|---|---|---|
| 1911 | During the last of the Chinese dynasties, revolution spreads among China's provinces and brings an end to the Ch'ing Dynasty and the power of the Manchus, which prevailed for over 250 years. | |
| 1912 | The Chinese Republic is established on January 1 with Sun Yat-sen as president; he soon resigns in favor of Yüan Shih-k'ai and takes command of the Kuomintang, which he founded in 1905. | Weili's Gung-gung (grandfather) loses his government job and dies. |
| 1915 | A treaty between China and Japan establishes Japanese dominance in Shantung, Manchuria, and Inner Mongolia. | |
| 1916 | President Yüan Shih-k'ai dies; warlords return to power in many provinces. | |
| 1918 | | Jiang Weili (Winnie) is born in Shanghai. |
| 1919 | | Hulan (Helen) is born near Loyang. |
| 1923 | Sun Yat-sen reorganizes Kuomintang with support from a still-small Communist Party. | |
| 1925 | Sun Yat-sen dies. Chiang Kai-shek takes over the leadership | Weili's mother disappears, abandoning Weili. Weili is sent |

of the Kuomintang.

1926    The Communists call a general strike in Shanghai, overthrowing local warlords. Chiang turns on the Communists, killing thousands.

1927    Chiang Kai-shek establishes a new Nationalist government at Nanking, challenged by Communists.

1931    The Japanese occupy the Chinese province of Manchuria and control two other provinces in northeast China. Mao Tse-tung creates the Chinese Communist Republic in Jiangxi province, where millions of Chinese are without means of earning a living.

1932    Japan invades and bombs Shanghai but is later forced to abandon it. Japan creates the puppet state of Manchukuo from Manchuria. Henry Pu-yi (the "last emperor" of China) is abducted from Tientsin and made Manchukuo's puppet emperor.

1934    As many as 100,000 Communists under Mao Tse-tung and Zhu De begin the "long march" of 6,000 miles north from Jiangxi to escape the Kuomintang.

1935    Perhaps 8,000 survive the long march and arrive in Shaanxi. Mao Tse-tung is chosen as the Communist party leader after the success of the long march.

1937    The Chinese Communists and the Kuomintang join together to fight the Japanese, their

to live in an uncle's house on Tsungming Island. She attends a boarding school in Shanghai. Weili continues attending the missionary school in Shanghai.

Weili meets and marries Wen Fu, who joins the air force to become a pilot. They move to common enemy. Claire Chennault retires from the U.S. Army in April to become an air training advisor to the Chinese government (June). The Chinese repel a Japanese attempt to take some bridges near Peking (July). China declares a War of Resistance against Japan, now invading Shanghai (August). Chiang Kai-shek is named Commander-in-Chief of all of China's armed forces. The first offensive air mission over Shanghai (August 14) accidentally kills almost 1,000 civilians. Shanghai falls (November). Capital moved from Nanking to Hankow (December). U.S. ships are sunk near Nanking, which falls with enormous destruction and the massacre of many thousands.

Hangchow for pilot training, where Weili meets Hulan. The air force flies its first disastrous mission over Shanghai. The pilots are moved almost immediately to Yangchow and then to Nanking, where Weili and Hulan experience *taonan* when Japanese planes fly over the marketplace. They are sent from Nanking on the long trip to Kunming in southwest China. Along the way, they hear the news about the destruction of Nanking.

1938    Chennault sets up an air training base at Kunming. The capital is moved from Hankow to Chungking. The Japanese attack China's industrial heartland in the Wuchang-Hankow area. After five months of battle, the Japanese take Hankow and Canton, the last major Chinese port, effectively cutting China off from supplies by sea (October). The 700-mile Burma Road is completed as a supply road to China from the railhead at Lashio in Burma to Kunming.

Weili's first child, Mochou, is born dead in Kunming. Wen Fu wrecks a jeep, killing a woman passenger and losing sight in one eye.

1939    In the new capital of Chungking, 8,000 are killed in two days of bombing (May). The Japanese are defeated at Changsha, their first real defeat (October).

Weili's second child, Yiku, is born in Kunming.

*hits her* ↓

| | | |
|---|---|---|
| 1940 | In July, the British close Rangoon, Burma (under British rule), to incoming Chinese supplies to avoid confrontation with the Japanese. (Britain had to focus its military attention on the Germans gathering on the English Channel.) The effect was the same as closing the Burma Road. In October, the British reopened Rangoon, and the Burma Road flourished again with military supplies for China. | Yiku dies after abuse by Wen Fu and convulsions from illness. Danru, Weili's third child and first son, is born. |
| 1941 | Chennault's Flying Tigers (an American Volunteer Group) set up headquarters in Kunming. The Japanese bomb Pearl Harbor, Hawaii, and the U.S. declares war on Japan. | The Japanese bomb Kunming repeatedly while Wen Fu and Jiaguo are in Chungking training people for defense and setting up an early warning system. Back in Shanghai, the Japanese take control of Jiang Sao-yen's business. He appears to be a traitor to the Chinese. At a Christmas dance in Kunming, sponsored by the Americans, Weili meets Jimmy Louie, who gives her the name "Winnie." Weili makes her first futile attempt to leave Wen Fu. |
| 1942 | | Weili becomes pregnant several times and aborts the fetus each time. |
| 1944 | Japanese defeats by U.S. forces in the Pacific halt their advances in China. The Japanese are gradually pushed back in China. Friction between Chinese Nationalists and Chinese Communists increases. War has weakened and corrupted the Nationalists, while mobilizing and strengthening the Communists. | |

| | | |
|---|---|---|
| 1945 | Attempts between Nationalists and Communists to settle differences fail. The U.S. drops the first atomic bomb on Hiroshima and Nagasaki, Japan, ending the war for China as well as for the Allies. Japan surrenders (August). | Weili, Wen Fu, and Danru travel back to Shanghai to her father's house. Soon after, Wen Fu's family moves into the house and takes control of the household. |
| 1946 | All-out war is declared between the Chinese Communists and Nationalists. Communists seize territory wherever they can. | Weili and Danru visit the aunts on Tsungming Island and get Peanut's address. Weili accidentally meets Jimmy Louie, finds Peanut and gets the final motivation to leave Wen Fu. She moves in with Jimmy. |
| 1947 | Open civil war erupts between Nationalists and Communists. | Weili and Jimmy send Danru north out of Wen Fu's reach. Danru dies in an epidemic. Weili is arrested, tried, and imprisoned. Jimmy loses his government job and is ordered to leave China. He goes to San Francisco. |
| 1948 | The Communists denounce U.S. aid to Chiang Kai-shek. Martial law is declared by Chiang. | Weili continues her term in prison. Jimmy studies to become a Christian minister. |
| 1949 | The Communists take control of Peking, Nanking, Shanghai, and Canton and proclaim the People's Republic of China. Chiang resigns as President, Mao is elected Chairman, and Chou En-lai is appointed Premier. The U.S. consul is ejected. | Newly married to Kuang An and expecting his baby, Hulan visits Weili in prison. Auntie Du arranges for Weili's release (April). Weili wires Jimmy, and he tells her to come to the U.S. Before leaving, she tricks Wen Fu into signing divorce papers. He tracks Weili down and rapes her at gunpoint. She escapes and leaves China the next day to go to Jimmy in California, just five days before the Communists take over Shanghai and halt emigration. |
| 1950 | The Nationalist government flees to Formosa (Taiwan). The | Pearl Louie is born in California. |

| | |
|---|---|
| | U.S. orders all consulates closed on mainland China. The U.S. is on the verge of war with China. |
| 1952 | Samuel Louie is born. |
| 1953 | Winnie and Jimmy help Hulan and her family get to America from Formosa. |
| 1964 | Jimmy Louie dies, and fourteen-year-old Pearl refuses to accept it. Together, Winnie and Helen open a flower shop in Chinatown, San Francisco. |
| 1975 | Pearl Louie marries Phil Brandt. |
| 1982 | Tessa Brandt is born. |
| 1983 | Pearl is diagnosed with multiple sclerosis. |
| 1987 | Cleo Brandt is born. |
| 1989 | Wen Fu dies in China of heart disease. |
| 1990 | Auntie Du dies in a bus accident. The family gathers for Bao-bao's engagement party and Auntie Du's funeral. Winnie finally confides to Pearl the story of her life, and Pearl tells her mother about her multiple sclerosis. |

# CRITICAL COMMENTARIES

## Introductory Note

The entire novel is narrated in *first person* by two central characters: Pearl and her mother, Winnie.

- **Chapters 1 and 2** are narrated by Pearl Louie Brandt, a contemporary Asian-American woman in her forties. The events she describes are mostly in present time and are narrated in *present tense.*
- **Chapters 3 and 4** are narrated by Pearl's Chinese mother, Winnie Louie, as she begins to think about her family, her past, and her need to confide in her daughter.
- **Chapters 5 through 24** are narrated as if being told by

Winnie to Pearl. This is the story of Winnie's life, most of it described through *flashbacks*, with occasional *asides* and *editorial comments* by the narrator. (Winnie's Chinese name in most of these flashbacks is Weili.)

- **Chapter 25** is in present time again, narrated by Pearl immediately following her mother's story.
- **Chapter 26** is narrated by Winnie in the days after she tells her story to Pearl.

## CHAPTERS 1 & 2

In January 1990, Pearl Brandt's mother, Winnie Louie, has convinced Pearl of her family duty to attend the engagement dinner for a Kwong cousin—a member of the extended Louie-Kwong family. The visit requires Pearl, her husband Phil, and their two young daughters to drive fifty miles from San Jose to San Francisco for the banquet at a restaurant. They must also stay overnight for the funeral of Grand Auntie Du to be held the day after the party.

Here, we meet all the major present-day characters and learn something of their individual concerns, fears, and hopes:

- The communication between Pearl and her mother, Winnie, is strained and awkward. Each readily misinterprets what the other is saying. Pearl does not seem able to confide in or talk companionably with her mother.
- Pearl has been diagnosed with **multiple sclerosis** (MS), but has not been able to tell her gabby mother and has finally given up trying.
- Pearl and her husband, Phil, both seem apprehensive about the MS; Pearl, a speech clinician in the public school system, dislikes gestures of sympathy from others. Phil, a pathologist, tries to minimize the stress in their home lives while informing himself about medical advances in the treatment of MS and performing periodic "safety checks" on Pearl's reflexes and strength.
- Helen Kwong has been Winnie's friend for over fifty years and, with Winnie, has co-owned the Ding Ho Flower Shop in Chinatown for twenty-five years, ever since the death of Winnie's husband, Jimmy Louie. Helen is referred to as Winnie's sister-in-law by a previous marriage.

- Helen has learned about Pearl's MS. To Pearl, Helen reveals her own brain tumor, which the doctors call benign, but which she believes is terminal. Helen urges Pearl to tell her mother about the multiple sclerosis. If she doesn't, Helen herself will do so in the clearing of the air that customarily accompanies the Chinese New Year.
- Auntie Du was Helen's aunt, but Winnie is the one who has looked out for her interests for many years. At ninety-seven, energetic Auntie Du was injured in a bus accident and died of a concussion in the hospital, after seeming to be on the mend.

Auntie Du's Buddhist funeral is confusing to the Brandts, especially to the children, whose arguments result in their removal from the ceremony by their Caucasian father. Amid the smell of incense, whirring video camera, wails of hired mourners, and chants of saffron-robed monks, the assembled family achieves little genuine mourning. Pearl begins crying during the ceremony. Winnie and Pearl both realize that Pearl is finally crying for her father, Jimmy Louie, who died over twenty-five years earlier; at that time, Pearl refused to grieve.

Auntie Du has left to Pearl her table-top Chinese altar to the Kitchen God, who watches over everyone's behavior, deciding "who deserves good luck, who deserves bad." Winnie tells Pearl and her family the story of the Kitchen God and his wife.

## Commentary

The novel begins in January 1990 in California, mostly in San Francisco. Amy Tan opens her novel on an amusing and disturbing **montage**—the conjunction of a betrothal and a funeral. The **thematic** alliance of love and death reduces life to its simplest terms and introduces the **conflicts** that lurk beneath the surface actions of people who conceal their true feelings.

The gathering of the Kwong and Louie families for a cousin's engagement banquet and the funeral of Auntie Du become the background against which are revealed excuses, animosities, old grievances, and regrets. A **kaleidoscope** of scenes pairs mother with daughter, aunt with niece, Caucasian son-in-law with Chinese brother-in-law, grouchy children with a loving "Ha-bu"—all weaving through the testy relationship between two crafty, strongly bonded septuagenarians, Winnie and Helen.

The novel's **exposition** bursts with examples of the **theme** of *illusion versus reality*. Interlacing the **action** of seemingly congenial family behavior are deceptions and discrepancies such as these:

- Roger, a thirty-year-old man whose two previous marriages have failed, answers to Bao-bao, meaning "precious baby."
- Auntie Du appears unhurt in a bus accident, then dies of an undetected concussion.
- Pearl carries out her duty to her extended family with seeming grace, but actually with reluctance. A Chinese-American woman, Pearl is so removed from China that she recognizes few Chinese sentences or written characters.
- Pearl is privately troubled about her multiple sclerosis and her future with it, although she shrugs off expressions of concern and has not yet told her mother that she has the disease.
- Pearl's husband, Phil, talks around the subject of her MS and yet tries to protect his wife from stress by denying her intellectual need to debate and challenge ideas.
- Helen worries that she is dying of a brain tumor diagnosed as benign.
- Roger serves as a pallbearer for Auntie Du after suggesting that his family sue the bus company for a million dollars.
- Mourners—some of them paid—wear the face of sorrow, and families attempt to follow old social and religious patterns that no longer have meaning.
- Pearl's children wonder if the body at the funeral is a woman sleeping at the dinner table. Distracted, their concerns quickly turn to what kind of ice cream they will have when they leave the funeral.
- Pearl openly expresses grief at Auntie Du's funeral—grief which is actually for her father and has been long suppressed. This emotional **catharsis** suggests that her mourning is tainted with self-pity and fear of her own future incapacitation and death from MS.

While revealing such thematic material, Tan does not intend for her characters to mire themselves in recriminations or for her readers to slog through a grief-sodden terrain. Anguish and sorrow are masterfully **balanced** by lighter moments such as these:

- Cleo's reference to wanting to see dingbats in the zoo after her father uses the word to refer to Pearl's cousin Mary

- Helen's reference to Pearl's "multiple neurosis" as well as her own "B-9" tumor
- Roger's reference to "pumping iron" as a warm-up for pallbearing
- Uncle Henry's videotaping of the funeral, including both the postured entrance and the awkward exit of Pearl's children
- Winnie's comment that the women hired as mourners make a better living that way than if they cleaned houses
- the funeral banner that falls and drapes itself across Auntie Du's body
- Winnie's pride in her skill of saving money on tofu and toilet paper.

The Chinese legend of the Kitchen God and his wife, as told by Winnie to the Brandts at the end of Chapter 2, provides a partial parallel for the story of Winnie's own life, which will become the main narrative of the novel.

---

(Here and in the following chapters, difficult allusions, words, and phrases are explained.)

- **herbal medicine**   Records dating to the eighteenth century B.C. indicate that Chinese healers depended on herbal cures to defeat disease and restore balance and energy through a holistic regimen of acupuncture and herbs. Herbal remedies now draw a widening range of Western supporters and users.

- **concussion**   an injury to the brain or spinal cord resulting from a sharp blow or fall.

- **multiple sclerosis (MS)**   a chronic nerve disease, of unknown origin and as yet incurable, that gradually destroys the myelin insulating coat on the surface of nerve fibers. As it progresses to different parts of the nervous system, it may be accompanied by such symptoms as tremors, lack of coordination, unsteady gait, mental disorientation, impaired vision, numbness, and paralysis. Onset may be followed by decades of remission; emotional trauma can trigger a relapse. However, average life expectancy for the MS patient today is more than thirty-five years after its onset and can be extended through systematic self-care and adjustment of lifestyle. Also, medication and therapy may lessen its severity and improve the individual's mental outlook.

- **art deco**   a boldly geometric style in architecture and home furnishings characterized by clean lines; often constructed from chrome, glass, or shiny plastic. Art deco—a brash break with traditional materials and classic lines—dominated the fashion world in the 1920s. Pearl's bedroom furniture, dating from her teens, is so out-of-date that it appears to have cycled back into style.

- **pop-beads** an inexpensive costume jewelry common in the 1960s, made of individual soft plastic beads the wearer can link together into necklaces and bracelets of any desired length—or, in this case, into letters of the alphabet.

- **ancestor memorials** shrines to deceased family members maintained out of deep respect, filial piety, and family duty. Honor and service to ancestors require gifts and periodic cleaning of burial sites. Relatives living away from ancestor memorials may contract with local professional mourners to carry out their family responsibilities. (Note: In Chapter 19, Shanghai's patriots retaliate against those who collaborated with the Japanese by defacing family grave plots.)

- **Buddhist funerals** The Chinese Buddhist ritual described here involves preparing the body for the afterlife, providing food for the journey, inscribing lucky characters on the casket or on parchment scrolls, mourning, and intoning the mantra, a meditational chant.

- **Cantonese, Shanghainese, Mandarin** dialects of the **Sino-Tibetan**-language family, second only in number of speakers to the Indo-European language family (which includes English). The many dialects of Chinese serve over seven hundred million speakers from China, Southeast Asia, and Tibet. **Mandarin** serves the largest number of speakers as the standard written and spoken language—over ninety percent of all Chinese use it. **Shanghainese**, a dialect within Mandarin, is spoken in the environs of Shanghai, and **Cantonese** is the dialect of Canton (now Guangzhou), Southern China, and Hong Kong.

- **Christmas crèche** a traditional scene representing the birth of Jesus in an animal stall in Bethlehem, often displayed by Christians during the celebration of Christmas; a crèche usually includes the figures of Jesus, Mary and Joseph, and often angels, shepherds, three kings, and animals.

- **a Chinese version of Freud** Sigmund Freud was the founder of psychoanalysis. His name now suggests the existence of hidden reasons and causes for an individual's behavior.

- **Shiites** a political wing of the Islamic faith that maintains allegiance to Ali, a cousin and successor to Mohammed, whom less dogmatic Muslims consider the only prophet of Allah, or God. Iraq is the stronghold of the *shia*, or a party composed of Shiites.

- **Chinese New Year** a fifteen-day Chinese festival that occurs between January 21 and February 19. The focus of celebration is the payment of debts, housecleaning, and the ending of quarrels to prepare the way for a peaceful new year.

- **the Holy Ghost** In Christian religious doctrine, God is a **Trinity**—the unity of Father, Son, and Holy Ghost (or Holy Spirit).

- **Amitaba** the spiritual guide summoned by the Buddhist monks to escort Auntie Du from her earthly existence to the afterlife. Amitaba is a Buddha who rules over paradise while enjoying endless bliss. (Note: The cry to Amitaba recurs in Chapter 12 as shoppers in the Nanking marketplace drop to the ground during the bombing and call on the heavenly guide to end their pain and terror.)

- **Cultural Revolution** In the mid-1960s, the Chinese Communist Party under Chairman Mao Tse-tung demoted or purged from the Party all complacent, disloyal, or weak party members. The revitalization of hardline communism, often referred to as the Cultural Revolution, was led by the Red Guard and fueled by the fanaticism of Mao's wife, Chiang Ch'ing, ultimately degenerating into terrorism, victimization, torture, murder, and anarchy. In 1967, under internal and international duress for human rights violations, Mao curbed the Red Guard's power to avenge private animosities in the name of Party enhancement.

- **Zen** a mystical form of Buddhism that dates from the *Tao Te Ching* (The Way of Life), a brief sixth-century B.C. religious and ethical manual urging seekers to follow the path of virtue. The originator of Taoist study was Lao Tzu. Today, various forms of Zen influence most of the Orient. The study of Zen has also expanded in many parts of the West, including the United States.

- **potstickers** a slang name for steamed *dim sum*, a savory Cantonese dumpling used as an appetizer or canapé.

- **tofu** a smooth, white soybean curd, a staple in Oriental cooking because of its availability, digestibility, high protein content, and adaptability to numerous recipes, including soups, stir fry, main dishes, and salads.

- **See's candies** a brand of chocolates especially popular in California.

## CHAPTERS 3 & 4

Simple day-to-day events in Winnie's ongoing love/hate relationship with Helen stir up scattered memories of her early life and its interweaving with China's political upheaval in the 1920s, 1930s, and 1940s. She believed that immigration to California would relieve her of the many secrets and deceptions that helped her deal with her crisis-filled life in China.

After immigrating to America, Winnie managed to live without new lies until 1953, when her longtime friend Helen claimed repayment of an old debt, asking for Winnie's help in getting Helen and her family from Formosa to the U.S. So once more Winnie lied, stating that Helen was a half-sister, the offspring of one of her father's other wives. Then, being the wife of a minister, Winnie did not want to reveal her father's polygamy, so she recast Helen as her sister-in-law, once married to one of Winnie's brothers.

Helen Kwong is *not* related to Winnie, even by marriage. Winnie acknowledges that the relationship with Helen reflects genuine sibling rivalry, even though the two women are kin only in the lies they perpetuate and the trivial arguments they relish.

Winnie (whose Chinese name is Weili) was first married in China to an abusive, unprincipled man, Wen Fu, before she came to the United States and married Jimmy Louie. She has lived in continual fear of Wen Fu's reappearance in her life. Helen knows about Wen Fu and about most of Winnie's early life. Helen suddenly threatens to tell all their shared secrets before the Chinese New Year unless Winnie takes responsibility for making her own disclosures.

Helen tells Winnie there is no more need for all the secrets they have kept from their families. Through a letter from a mutual friend in China, Helen has learned that the despised Wen Fu died in China just the previous month. Winnie has difficulty absorbing the news and its impact on her life.

Uncertain how to deal with Helen's threat to reveal all, Winnie cleans her house, awakening memories of her family life in America through discovery of such items as an old copy of *Playboy* she had ordered her son Samuel to destroy, initials carved on Pearl's old dressing table, and Pearl's childhood treasure box containing a schoolgirl letter, an announcement of a Sadie Hawkins Day Dance, and a marked-up religious card from Jimmy Louie's funeral.

Facing the alienation that separates her from Pearl, Winnie acknowledges that she has always loved her daughter more than she loved her son. She admits to herself that she owes Pearl the truth about her own life, including the terrible fact that Wen Fu rather than Jimmy Louie is Pearl's father.

# Commentary

Beginning in Chapter 3, Tan shifts the narrative **point of view** from Pearl to the strong voice of her mother, Winnie. In these two chapters, Winnie's thoughts touch on an amazing range of events from her life, creating a fragile **framework** for the novel's **focus**—the story of a Chinese child from a wealthy background whose mother abandons her, leaving her devalued and ignored in a feudal household from which she must make her way into a world once defined by centuries of imperialism and warlords, then challenged by internal political divisions, invading Japanese, and communism.

Winnie maintains that her best friend—and persistent **foil**—Helen Kwong, has inborn luck, a quality that has seemingly dried up in Winnie because of "the fate that was given me, the choices I took, the mistakes that are mine." Central to Winnie's philosophy is the distinction between *having* luck and *making* luck. To Winnie, marriage to Wen Fu foreshadowed a long slide into physical pain, spiritual torpor, and diminished will. Yet, when seen from the point of view of growth, Winnie's inner worth blossoms when she is told by the sisterhood supporting her that only she herself can create her own good fortune.

In assessing her life and luck, Winnie recalls an incident years ago that changed the way she looked at life. Standing outside Jimmie Louie's church when Pearl and Samuel were very young, greeting members of Jimmie's Christian congregation after a Sunday service, Winnie was introduced to Lin, a man from her uncle's village whom she might have married, now a successful doctor. Overcome by heat as well as embarrassment at recalling a childhood faux pas, Winnie felt the fusion of "my past, my life today, my first husband, my second husband, Lin"—and then she fainted in front of everyone. Later, when she started to consider how things might have been had she married Lin, she had a sudden insight and "from that day on, I began to look at everything in my life two ways, the way it happened, the way it did not."

Her subsequent telling of her life story reflects that two-sided philosophy, occasionally cultivating fantasies that breed regret. Now, in her seventies, Winnie reevaluates her experiences with Lin, Wen Fu, and Jimmy Louie, and she concludes that she was grateful for a good second marriage, but was "never completely happy."

- **smallpox** an acute, contagious disease—now largely controlled through vaccination—that often leaves the face pitted or scarred with marks called pock marks.

- **lose face** to suffer social disgrace or embarrassment. The concept of preserving outward appearances at all costs is a controlling social mechanism throughout the novel, often explaining why Tan's characters go to such lengths following age-old traditions and rituals to avoid shaming themselves. For example, receivers of gifts open them in private to avoid revealing disappointment and thus embarrassing both the givers and receivers.

- **Horse year** Each full year of the Chinese calendar is symbolized by one of twelve traditional animals. The Horse years in this century took place, for example, in 1918, 1930, 1942, and 1954 on the Western calendar. Winnie characterizes a Horse year as a time "when people stamped their feet and became reckless."

- **Kuomintang** The word means "national people's party" in Chinese. In 1912, **Dr. Sun Yat-sen** directed this political party. Suppressed by China's new president, the party twice tried to establish revolutionary governments in Canton. In 1925, after Sun's death and considerable interparty strife, the Kuomintang passed into the control of **General Chiang Kai-shek** and his Nationalists. By 1950, ousted from mainland China by the Communists, the Kuomintang governed the Nationalist Chinese on Taiwan for many years under Chiang Kai-shek.

- **Marxist** a Communist and follower of Karl Marx, the philosopher and writer whose *Communist Manifesto* (1848) proclaimed collectivism—the sharing of wealth among all citizens—as a more equitable social, economic, and political system than either capitalism or monarchy.

- **Formosa** a shortened form of the Portuguese phrase *ihla formosa*, meaning "beautiful island." It was given by sixteenth-century Portuguese traders to the island, which is one hundred fifteen miles southeast of mainland China. This island, now called Taiwan, was under Japanese control from 1895 to 1945.

- **Taiwan** means "terraced bay" in Chinese. In 1949, Communist forces drove Chiang Kai-shek and China's nationalists to the island, where they established the Republic of China—in contrast to the *People's* Republic of China, which is Communist mainland China.

- **Kowloon** a part of the British colony of Hong Kong on the southeast coast of China.

- **Sadie Hawkins Day** The first Saturday after November 11, this annual event was created by cartoonist Al Capp in 1939 in his American hillbilly comic strip *Li'l Abner*; it is the day when single women chase bachelors in order to get husbands. In the 1940s, this translated into the American life-style as a day or an event when girls could invite boys to escort them to a dance or a movie.

## CHAPTERS 5–7

After summoning Pearl to her on a pretext of heart pain, Winnie begins telling her daughter a story she has incubated for forty years—the story of her life in China as "Weili."

Winnie finds her heart still emotionally torn with longing for her beautiful mother, who left their Shanghai home one morning in early 1925, when Weili was six, never to return. She remembers the room she shared with her mother in their fancy house, where they lived with Weili's wealthy father, Jiang Sao-yen, and his three other wives. She recalls in detail a day in 1925: she overhears her mother and father arguing, probably about her mother's status in the family. Later in the day, Weili and her mother take an extensive excursion alone—most unusual—to downtown Shanghai, walking around (her mother usually carried her), window shopping, attending a movie, and generally enjoying the sights and sounds of the city.

The same evening at home, her mother spends time showing Weili a new embroidery stitch, teaching her to count her fingers and toes, and displaying jewelry that will all be Weili's some day.

When Weili awakes the next morning, her mother has disappeared, leaving many questions in Weili's mind: Where did she go? Did she leave with the man she met at the movie theater? Why did she leave Weili behind? Who will look after her now?

The decision about Weili's immediate future is made by some unnamed power—perhaps her father and his third wife, the sensible San Ma. As a result, about a week after her mother's disappearance, Weili travels two hours by motorboat up the Huangpu River to Tsung-ming Island. Here she joins the household of her father's younger brother and his two wives, "Old Aunt" and "New Aunt" to Weili.

Remorse, yearning, and gossipy nonsense tangle the slender threads in Weili's memory of a mother who abandoned her daughter to free herself from a loveless marriage. She remembers her mother "ten thousand different ways." From the perspective of 1990, Winnie looks back on seven decades of imaginings about her mother's fate—as a drowning victim, a nunnery conscript, a romantic newlywed, a rebellious Marxist, or an unmourned corpse buried at the village of Mouth of the River. She has never been able to anchor the image of her strong-willed, fashion-conscious mother to a final fate or resting place.

Returning to 1925, we see Weili spending almost twelve years either in a missionary boarding school in Shanghai (never seeing her father) or in her uncle's house on Tsungming Island, which is ruled by the two aunts, who either ignore her or carp at her. In that house, Weili never enjoys the status of being a family member, ranking lower even than a perennial guest. For example, she finally has no choice: she has to embarrass her aunts in front of others before they will replace her worn-out clothes. Weili's younger cousin, nicknamed "Peanut," and Peanut's two younger brothers get the attention in the family.

In early 1937, before the Chinese New Year, Weili accompanies her overdressed, overpainted cousin Peanut and the two boys to the local marketplace. As part of the holiday celebration, vendor stalls sell special foods, toys, candies, hair ornaments, and much more. Fortune tellers nourish dreams of a bright year ahead, and Peanut spends more than her share of the money they have been given to pay for a fortune about what kind of husband she will have.

Actors in the marketplace perform a silly play and beg for money to support a local charity. One bold, flamboyant actor is Wen Fu, the eldest son of a family with an overseas business. He delights the two boy cousins and becomes attentive to Peanut, apparently aware that hers is the wealthiest family on the island. He even ferries her home from the marketplace in a borrowed wheelbarrow.

In the days that follow the 1937 Chinese New Year celebration, Wen Fu continues his wooing of Peanut with secret messages and meetings, arranged with Weili's disapproval and assistance. However, when a marriage is finally proposed through Auntie Miao, the local matchmaker, the offer by the Wen parents is for Wen Fu to marry Weili (who is a daughter of the successful textile magnate Jiang Sao-yen) rather than Peanut (the daughter of Jiang's less successful brother). Suddenly, Weili begins to dream of a home among loving family members.

Seeing herself betrayed, Peanut becomes physically and verbally abusive to Weili, who remembers that the fortune teller predicted Peanut would lose her local suitor to someone else. Neither of them are as yet aware of how greedy and heartless the Wens are.

Needing her father's approval of the marriage, Weili's aunts take her to Shanghai for a visit with her father. He agrees to the marriage and gives her a substantial financial dowry for her personal use. San Ma, her father's third wife, then takes her on a seven-day spree of dowry shopping, buying everything from triple dressers and armoires to intimate garments, tubs for personal hygiene, and ten pairs of silver chopsticks. Although the purchases seem very generous, Weili later learns that San Ma had purchased items for a much larger dowry—"five times bigger"—for another of Jiang's daughters. Weili concludes that her father must be aware of the Wens' poor reputation and that he must not have thought much of her to marry her to Wen Fu.

As an omen of how the Wens will treat her, most of her purchased dowry is taken by members of the Wen family as their own or sold overseas by the Wens to get the money. Her hidden sets of silver chopsticks and her dowry in the bank become her only possessions of value.

## Commentary

The loss of her mother in childhood is the dramatic source for many of Winnie's thoughts and feelings. According to Amy Tan's reflective article "Lost Lives of Women" (*Life*, April 1991), her own concept of Chinese "loss of face" began at home with the study of a photograph taken in 1924 showing female members of her family in mourning. After Daisy Tan confided the facts of the rape of her mother, Jingmei, and her subsequent subjection to the role of concubine, Daisy burst into an emotional defense:

"How can you understand?" she said, suddenly angry. "You did not live in China then. You do not know what it's like to have no position in life. I was her daughter. We had no face! We belonged to nobody! This is a shame I can never push off my back." The outcry echos the shame and anchorless emotion of Weili, whose treatment by her uncle and his two wives remind her daily that she is a burdensome relative living off their charity and condescending good will.

Tan herself traveled to China and followed the Huangpu River from Shanghai—the route Weili took after her father dispatched her to Uncle's house on Tsungming Island—to her grandmother's place of exile. She wrote in "Watching China" (*Glamour*, September 1987), "I can only imagine what has happened to my family in China."

Destiny, another key in this novel, weaves in and out of events like the dragon procession that concludes the Chinese New Year celebration. Pre-Communist China's superstitions play active roles in the characters' lives—mythical cures, curses, whimsical gods, spirit money, seers, lucky days, and other forms of numerology. For example, Weili overhears the fortune teller shaping marriage predictions to Peanut's wishes and reactions, "chasing away" the local man she was supposed to marry, sending him to someone else, and promising Peanut wealth with a man farther away. Later, Weili cannot explain (except through destiny) the transference of the ill luck that skips Peanut—that is, marriage to Wen Fu—into the catastrophe that overwhelms and dominates much of Weili's adult life.

For several pages, the story takes on the trappings of a **fable**. After Auntie Miao applies her mercenary skills to a satisfactory—that is, a mutually profitable—union between the Wens and Jiangs, the buoyant, reassuring visions of "happily ever after" transform Weili (her uncle's out-of-favor foster child) into the Cinderella of the moment. During her reunion with her dignified, refined father to discuss the marriage offer and an appropriate dowry, Weili allows herself a recapitulation of scenes from her childhood home and a sensual taste/touch/smell/look session in the room so shadowed by ill fortune that no one risks fate by moving in.

Even bittersweet memories of her mother fail to daunt Weili's joy in her betrothal. Although obviously forewarned, Weili pays allegiance to the same patriarchal system that held her mother in bondage and forced her to finally value her own freedom over her duties as a mother. Perhaps the young Weili believes her mother's story was a fluke, a rare example of a headstrong, Westernized, overeducated wife too sure of herself to allow a man to do her thinking for her.

Weili and San Ma's seven-day dowry-buying spree reads like a **tale** about a starving beggar following a philanthropist to a banquet table and sampling at will from a rich man's birthright. So long deprived of the family attention that builds self-esteem, Weili grabs at every bauble, every purchase that revalidates her inner worth. Like a pre-marital counselor, San Ma explains the importance of each item, such as the intimate garments and the special tubs in which she should wash to keep her body sweet and appealing to her groom.

The **dramatic irony** of the seventh day of shopping presents a wide-eyed bride-to-be handling the "Chinese silver, pure, soft silver, just like money you can exchange" and ignoring San Ma's dealings with the clerk over table settings to serve ten. Like man and wife in ideal matrimony, a pair of chopsticks in Weili's fingers are of equal length and value, mated with a silver chain to keep each from straying from the other. Mimicking her role as wife and nipping at imaginary morsels with heavy silver chopsticks—the only bridal gift that Weili will manage to save for herself—she actually clutches at nothing of true significance.

---

- **warlord**  a military leader who has assumed control of a province or a territory within a country—here, a province within China. Warlords sometimes individually waged war on one another and occasionally formed coalitions and alliances. In 1912, warlordism was replaced temporarily by popular nationalism. However, after the new president's death in 1916, regional warlords vied with each other for control of the central government. Most provinces continued under the control of local military commanders until the Communist unification in 1949. The collapse of the warlords in that year coincides with Weili's escape from her abusive husband, Wen Fu, who treated Weili as a feudal lord might treat his vassal, a virtual slave, always subject to the lord's peculiar whims.

- **English biscuits**  fancy crackers or cookies, usually packed in a decorative tin. These and other luxuries—the mirror, Western clothing, jewelry, a private room, servants, and freedom of movement—indicate that although Weili's mother was a "double second" wife, she still enjoyed being pampered.

- **chamber pot**  a portable container used primarily for nighttime urine.

- **Double Second**  Jiang's original second wife committed suicide out of humiliation when she was not promoted to first wife after the first wife died of tuberculosis. Thus, the place of "second wife" was considered a "bad luck spot" by the envious third, fourth, and fifth wives, San Ma, Sz Ma, and Wu Ma. Weili's mother allowed herself to become "Double Second." The argument overheard by Weili may have been her mother's attempt to become "first wife."

- **pedicab**  a three-wheeled taxi holding as many as three passengers and pedaled by the driver like a tricycle. The pedicab replaced the bulkier

**rickshaw**, in which the driver ran on foot while pulling the cab with long poles grasped under each arm.

- **fatty man**   Fatty Arbuckle (1887–1933), a stout, baby-faced comedian of the silent screen, once as popular as Charlie Chaplin.

- **armoire**   an oversized storage cabinet or wardrobe with heavy hardware, often double-hinged doors, ornate detailing, painted scenes, or gilded oriental motifs called *chinoiserie*.

- **Tsungming Island**   an island forty miles long and eight miles wide in the mouth of the Yangtze River, north of Shanghai. Now called Chungming, the island grew hundreds of years ago from a sandbar in Shanghai harbor, an estuary of the Yangtze and Huangpu rivers.

- **bound feet**   a cruel and ancient Chinese custom for shaping girls' feet, a tradition that extended into the nineteenth century among families raising daughters to be "ladies." Parents wrapped their daughters' feet with toes extended downward, stretching the instep and inhibiting the shaping of the arch. Later, these women had to walk carefully in light, birdlike steps, creating an impression of fragility and modesty.

- **Confucius**   Latinized spelling of the name K'ung fu-tzu (probably 551–478 B.C.), who served as an adviser to an influential ruler. When the ruler died, Confucius became an itinerant teacher and sage. Three important doctrines of Confucius include believing in benevolence (doing unto others as to yourself), acting with benevolence, and acting in accordance with propriety.

- **Manchus**   rulers of the Ch'ing (Ching) Dynasty—the last Chinese imperial family, which dates its lineage from Manchuria in 1644. Emperor Hsuan T'ung, the teenaged heir of the Manchus, abdicated and was forced into house arrest on February 12, 1912. A month later, Yüan Shih-k'ai became the president of the new Chinese republic. Later a young man of Manchurian ancestry, Henry Pu-yi, was made puppet head of Manchukuo, formerly Manchuria, by the occupying Japanese.

- **wedding sedan**   an ornate, enclosed ceremonial chair in which a prospective bride is concealed from view behind curtains and, like a gift in gorgeous wrappings, is borne to the groom-to-be in a joyful, colorful wedding procession.

- *Catch Her in the Ride*   what Winnie understands as the title of J. D. Salinger's *Catcher in the Rye*, a teenage classic of emotional turmoil and insecurity. This novel of a runaway boy who flees failure at a private school was considered a shocking novel in the 1950s and is still the periodic target of book banning.

- **the Rat year**   1924 (also 1936, 1948, and every twelfth year thereafter).

- **cinnabar red**   a gaudy vermilion red, named for the mineral of that color called cinnabar, a mercuric sulfide.

- **wonton**   noodle dough filled with a meat mixture, served either fried or boiled as dumplings in broth.

- **pomelo**   a ten-to-twenty-pound pear-shaped citrus fruit, native to Malaysia and Polynesia and resembling a grapefruit with its thick rind, pale yellow pulp, and tart juice.

- **twelve animals of the horoscope**   The Chinese horoscope is based on years rather than months like the Western horoscope. Each year is represented by one of the following animals: Rat, Ox, Tiger, Rabbit, Dragon, Snake, Horse, Sheep, Monkey, Rooster, Dog, and Boar.

- **begging bowls**   shallow bowls such as Buddhist monks keep as their only possessions and use to collect donations thought to buy favor for the donors in the afterlife.

- **concubine**   a woman kept in a household primarily as a sexual partner, not a wife; she is considered inferior to those who are wives.

- **yuan**   the Chinese monetary unit in the mid-1930s, equal to about fifty cents in American money at the time. Thus Weili's dowry of 4,000 yuan was the equivalent of about $2,000 then—perhaps $40-50,000 today.

## CHAPTERS 8–10

Before her wedding, Weili guesses that Peanut had already turned Wen Fu down, leaving her way clear for someone better (as told in her fortune). Now Peanut seems full of helpful suggestions about Weili's wedding.

Peanut passes on news about the unsavory business practices of the Wens, as well as a "sex story" to the sexually naive Weili. In the story, a young man dies because his penis becomes stuck in a woman whose overpowering *yin* destroys her groom, who has a lesser *yang*. Weili's casual glimpses of the tiny organs of her little boy cousins do not prepare her for the sight of Wen Fu's erect organ on their wedding night.

Relieved after telling Pearl about her wedding night ignorance and agony, Winnie turns her narrative to the circumstances under which she met Helen in 1937, one month after marrying Wen Fu.

While Chinese factions have been fighting among themselves,

the Japanese have taken over Chinese territory in the northeast. A new Chinese air force is being trained under an American advisor, General Claire Chennault, for air support to General Chiang Kai-shek, head of the Chinese Nationalists (Kuomintang). Using the false credentials of his deceased brother, Wen Fu has been accepted in the air force. With Weili in tow, Wen Fu reports for pilot training in Hangchow, about 100 miles southwest of Shanghai.

The living conditions in an old monastery at the training center are primitive, but the wives of the pilots make life as pleasant as possible. One of the wives is Hulan (later Helen), who is married to Long Jiaguo, Wen Fu's boss. Weili and Hulan become friends, even though their differences in family background, education, worldliness, and personality frequently put them at odds with each other.

When the thread of Winnie's story returns to the private details of her marriage, Winnie is not at ease discussing her husband's cruelty and vulgarity—even to her married daughter, Pearl. She prefaces her first account of Wen Fu's abuse with:

> So I will tell you what happened, although maybe not everything. Maybe I'll come to a part where I cannot say any more. And when that happens, you just have to imagine what happened. And then you should imagine it again and make it ten times worse.

Returning to 1937, Weili is surprised at how tolerant Jiaguo is of Hulan's nagging. Weili and Hulan have found a little outdoor pavilion in which to picnic, relax, and work embroidery in the hot summer afternoons and from which they have a glorious view of the surrounding area. One afternoon during a thunderstorm, Weili admits strange and erratic desires for food. After a few questions, Hulan convinces her she is pregnant. Weili is both uninformed and misinformed about pregnancy and birth. Hulan tells of her own unfortunate experience in her home near Loyang, trying to help her unmarried sister give birth. The baby's father had knocked the sister down in anger, precipitating the birth, and the sister died just before the baby was born dead. The man was Jiaguo, "so scared of my sister's curse that he married me," Hulan confides. Now Weili begins to understand his great patience with Hulan.

Wen Fu seems almost indifferent to the idea of a baby, and he continues to mistreat Weili. When Weili confides in Hulan, expecting commiseration, her trusted confidante reprimands her for not being more receptive to her husband's desires.

Suddenly they are told their husbands are flying out, and the wives rush to pack their husbands' clothes. They arrive at the air force base just in time to see their pilot-husbands getting final orders and then flying away, apparently into an air attack in which victory is anticipated.

## Commentary

In Chapter 8, Tan continues spacing segments of **oral transmission** with **digression** as Winnie relates to Pearl her quick metamorphosis from scared maiden to war bride and more gradual transformation to assertive woman. Tan reminds the reader, first, that Pearl knows nothing of her mother's burden of humiliation, guilt, regret, and worry for her daughter, and second, that the **autobiography** is a necessary account, narrated on her own terms lest Helen tells the story her way.

The joy of a mother-daughter relationship is central to the story with the sad irony that, unlike Weili, Pearl has a mother but, at this point in the action, does not avail herself of a loving, confiding relationship. Instead of bolstering one another, Pearl has drifted from intimacy into annoyance with her mother and self-absorption, while Winnie has turned to Helen, her annoying, competitive pseudo-sister.

Chapter 8 illustrates a **motif** of *surface value vs. genuine worth*—a reminder of the novel's **theme** of *illusion vs. reality*:

- Weili reflects on the happy days before the marriage, when Peanut's shallow worries concerned what kind of impression Weili would make on her father's clients and how much makeup the girls would wear, rather than the type of husband Wen Fu would make or what the prospects were for the couple's lasting contentment.
- Like the proverbial lamb to slaughter, Weili seems happy at the prospect of marriage and its escape, knowing little of the traditional sexual demands on a Chinese wife and even less of the evil nature of the man who waits to make her his property.
- A bountiful, festive atmosphere belies the two families' deceptions preceding the marriage that Weili is about to enter.
- Frequently uncharitable Old Aunt plays proxy for Weili's

44

beloved mother, giving Weili her mother's imperial jade earrings in secret.

- Days before the wedding, Peanut leads Weili to their secret spot for girlish confidences—the dilapidated greenhouse. Echoing the green of her mother's jade earrings and **foreshadowing** later references to Weili's green dress and coat, the greenhouse windows wink a promise of hope and refuge from adult chicanery and the extended family's callousness. Almost immediately, the green of hope withers as Peanut relates the news about the Wen family's sordid "garbage business," a disreputable method of milking foreigners of money by passing off Chinese shrines and paintings of ancestors to the Americans and British as treasured antiques.
- Weili is surprised that Wen Fu seems well liked by the other Chinese pilots, when in fact we learn later that they are afraid to cross him because they fear his anger.

Weili's developing fetus causes her to search for a certain food to satisfy her hunger, a yearning that parallels her longing for a loving family and a secure home, both lacking since her mother's disappearance. The urgent desire for food and love reminds her of her mother, "always wanting something more, never happy with what life had given me."

---

- **moxa**   the leaves of mugwort, also known as artemisia, or wormwood, which are burned in a treatment called moxibustion. Practitioners of Oriental herbal medicine use moxibustion as a curative, soothing therapy, muscle relaxant, or cauterizing agent.

- **eunuch**   a man who has been emasculated or castrated, often to make him a nonthreatening, asexual overseer of a harem or assemblage of royal or upperclass women.

- *yin*   the feminine element of Chinese philosophy—that is, receptive, cool, inactive, moist, and dark qualities.

- *yang*   the masculine element of Chinese philosophy—that is, aggressive, hot, active, dry, and bright qualities.

- **Madame Chiang**   Chiang Meiling Soong, a native of Shanghai and wife of **General Chiang Kai-shek**, the leader of the Kuomintang since 1925. In early 1937, Chiang turned air force matters over to Madame Chiang, charging her to eliminate its corruption, confusion, and incompetence. Mme. Chiang's American-educated brother, Dr. T.V. Soong, was Chiang's minister of finance and an enthusiatic supporter of using air power in China and of asking the U.S. to provide flight-training advisors. Herself educated at Wellesley College in Massachusetts, Mme. Chiang regularly used her knowledge and influence to aid her husband. Later, the first female to receive a commendation from the Chinese government, she wrote autobiographical studies of China's revolutionary years. On July 17, 1937, Chiang (sometimes referred to as "Generalissimo") convinced China's leaders of the need for massive defense and retaliation efforts, and on August 7, the War of Resistance against Japan was officially declared. On August 12, Chiang was named Commander-in-Chief of all Chinese armed forces. Two days later, August 14, was the date of China's first offensive air action at Shanghai, the sortie from Hangchow that takes flight at the end of Chapter 10.

- **Claire Chennault** A pioneer in American air pursuit tactics in World War I, he was nearing the age of forty-seven in 1937, when he found himself at odds with the U. S. Army Air Corps. He knew of the need for air expertise in China, so he retired as captain from U. S. Army and immediately went to China, where he became advisor to Chiang Kai-shek on air defense strategy. In 1941 in China, Chennault formed the Flying Tigers, an American volunteer group of skilled American pilots who were offered special bonuses to join the China mission. (Note: They celebrate early successes in Chapter 18 with the dance at which Weili meets Jimmy Louie.) Chennault was recalled to official duty in the Army Air Corps in 1942, when he officially headed the U.S. air task force in China. He finally retired in 1945 as a major general.

- **invisible body lice** crabs or scabies, both obtained through intimate contact, which Weili incorrectly links to the prurient itch of a lustful woman.

- **a late-night shooting up north in Peking** During the night of July 7–8, 1937, the Chinese repulsed a Japanese attempt to cross the Yungting River via two strategically critical bridges near Peking (then called Peiping, now called Beijing). However, on July 28, Peking fell to the Japanese.

### CHAPTERS 11 & 12

The tension and optimism of watching planes fly into combat from Hangchow give place to the dark news that the air fight over Shanghai harbor was disastrous for Jiaguo's unseasoned squadron, many of whom died in their planes. The woman reporting the losses has herself been widowed by this unsuccessful assault. Weili and Hulan argue (". . . our friendship took on four splits and five cracks") over their contradictory ways of responding to bad news and showing sympathy to others.

Later, while cutting out pieces of green fabric for a dress, Weili considers how she would react to news of Wen Fu's death and admits to herself she wishes this would happen. If Wen Fu were to die, she herself would choose her own replacement husband. The completed dress does not fit her pregnant body—"Stuck in my dress, stuck in my marriage, stuck with Hulan as my friend."

At the end of the summer (1937), the pilots move northward about 160 miles to Yangchow, and the wives follow them by boat, since many roads and rails have been blocked by the Japanese. Their quarters are again primitive, but Hulan cooks up mixtures for sealing the dirt floors and replastering the mud brick walls. With Hulan's welcome help, Weili prepares an expensive celebration dinner for her returning husband and his friends, the first of many such meals for the pilots. She spends her own dowry money for the elegant food, since Wen Fu spends all his air force salary on drinking and gambling.

Weili finds a special friend in shy and awkward Gan, an unmarried pilot. Privately he shares with her his fear of a ghost that first appeared to him as a boy eleven years ago during the last Tiger year (1926). The ghost promised to return for him before the next Tiger year (1938), but only after Gan experienced nine bad fates. Gan has already experienced eight of the predicted fates, and 1938 is only four months away. Winnie admits to Pearl that, with Gan, she "almost" felt love from a man and love for a man—new feelings for her.

Many of the pilots whom Weili and Wen Fu entertained were subsequently killed—but never Wen Fu, because he turned and flew away whenever an air battle was imminent. Jiaguo considers having him court-martialed for his cowardice, although Wen Fu always has a reason for fleeing the action. Gan is shot down and dies after two days of excruciating pain. Weili admits that after he died, "I claimed his love. He became like a ghost lover." Whenever Wen Fu shouts at her and abuses her, Weili thinks of Gan's kind words to her. She concludes that she herself was Gan's ninth fate, after which the ghost returned to claim him.

By winter 1937, war has ground down Jiaguo's squadron, which moves temporarily to Nanking, Chiang Kai-shek's new capital, less than fifty miles west of Yangchow. Almost immediately, they are told they will soon move again because of the approaching Japanese.

Wen Fu takes four hundred dollars of Weili's dowry money and buys a dilapidated old Fiat sports car with the top cut off. He glories in racing around the countryside, frightening Weili, ignoring her condition of being six months pregnant. With Jiaguo as his passenger, Wen Fu recklessly runs the car into a field and onto a rock pile that turns out to be a grave. The car catches fire and burns. Hearing the story from Hulan, Weili laughs hysterically at the irony of Wen Fu's recklessness, picturing the burning car as an offering to the dead pilot who was the car's former owner.

In Nanking, Weili telegraphs for more money—to be sent via Peanut in Shanghai this time. Then Weili and Hulan experience the terror of *taonan*, the untranslatable Chinese word that implies the mental lapse that precedes attempts to escape—the loss of connectedness to logic, to familiar faces, and to landmarks. The shoppers in the huge Nanking marketplace are menaced by several waves of low-flying Japanese planes which then disappear without dropping bombs. The frantic, scrambling mob shuffles through a swirl of propaganda leaflets dropped from the Japanese planes, offering good treatment in return for an unresisting populace. Weili loses contact with Hulan as they attempt to get away from a hurtling stampede of people fearing imminent invasion. In the chaos and fear that follow, Weili cries out for her mother and loses track of time. Sighting Weili's green coat, Hulan rescues her on a pedicab she has commandeered, beating off with a stick anyone who tries to take it from her.

They must leave Nanking the same day, and Weili forgets about the money she has sent for from her dowry.

## Commentary

Wartime brings the beginning of Weili's dependence on **sisterhood**—a strong motif of the book—reflected at the personal level in her appreciation of Hulan's fierce loyalty and pragmatism. The synergy of women working together results in a private bathhouse in their Hangchow quarters; in Yangchow, it powers an upgrading of spartan, vermin-infested surroundings. Weili begins to appreciate Hulan's homely skills, as well as her sincere regard for Weili's well-being, as illustrated in the escape from the Nanking marketplace.

Weili turns her attention from potential widowhood to the celebration of the returning pilots. For the first time in her life, Weili appears to be building self-esteem by taking the limelight as creator and hostess for splendid feasts. These efforts help compensate not only for her devaluation by the Jiangs and by Wen Fu, but also for the privations of war and the deaths of pilots in their compound: "You found any kind of excuse to live life as full as your stomach could hold." The hint of a stronger, more fulfilled Weili bodes well.

When the dinners expose Weili to the personalities of the other pilots, she cannot help contrasting the strutting, arrogant, deceitful Wen Fu with his foil, Gan—a shy, considerate, honest young man who unabashedly enjoys Weili's company. Encountering a variety of men for the first time in her sheltered life, Weili wonders, "Why didn't I know that I had a choice?" The centuries-old patriarchy and traditional female servitude not only deny access to self-awareness, self-actualization, learning, and use of skills, but to the crucial choices that determine a satisfactory marriage with a person of compatible tastes and temperament. Symbolizing the relationship between Weili and Gan, the two play a game of "chicken-feather ball" in the moonlight, gently batting back and forth a gamepiece as light as their friendship, which ends before it can develop into an emotion that calls for commitment from either of them.

Tan heightens the pathos of the potential love affair with Gan's ghost story, colored with mystical beliefs and numerology—for example, prophesying ghosts, the twelve-year cycle of zodiac animals, and the nine fates (life-affecting incidents). The number nine traditionally represents completion and finality.

As with many socially awkward incidents, Weili's joking response to Gan is a form of distancing and denial:
- the inability to embrace a man she wants to comfort and protect
- the inability to acknowledge a logical fear of death in battle
- the ability to laugh or tease, to lighten the fear brought on by the prophecy.

Yet, deeper than Weili's fear of loss is her fear of love, with its implicit threat of hurt. In her words, "I had never felt love from a man, or for a man. And that night I almost did. I felt the danger, that this was how you love someone . . . " After Gan's death, Weili wears the proper wifely mask to conceal her grief, but claims in retrospect,

"My heart hurt the same way as when I lost my mother. Only, I was not aching for a love I once had. I was regretting I never took it."

Through this experience, Weili advances to a more introspective stage, an improvement over her childish pattern of limiting herself to action/reaction. Her acceptance here parallels the assertion by Alfred Lord Tennyson, "It is better to have loved and lost/Than never to have loved at all" (Stanza 27 of *In Memoriam*).

Like her mother gazing for answers in the mirror, Weili arises from the humiliations of Wen Fu's bed and searches in her reflected face for the good that Gan saw in her. Her comforting memories of Gan are marred only by her conclusion that she and their incomplete relationship were his ninth bad fate, which cleared the way for the ghost's return to snatch him up.

---

- **the planes had flown late at night, toward the Shanghai harbor, swollen with Japanese boats** By November 1937, Japan had taken Manchuria, Korea, and the territory around Peking. The Japanese continued pressing down the coast to secure the important cities of Shanghai and Hong Kong.

- **Du Fu (sometimes, Tu Fu)** a Chinese poet (712–770 A.D.) from Tuling, Shensi Province, who lost his family in wartime upheaval, spent his life as a wanderer, and composed 1,405 stanzas.

- *tai-tai* a polite equivalent of the English "ma'am," directed to the mistress or lady of the house.

- **mah jong** a Chinese table game played by four people, originating in China in the nineteenth century, played in several different variations. Similar in some respects to rummy, it uses small tiles instead of cards. An Americanized version, mah-jongg, became popular in America during the 1920s.

- **catty** an Asian unit of weight weighing about 680 grams (1.36 pounds).

- **chicken-feather ball** an outdoor game comparable to badminton.

- **last time it was a Tiger year** 1926 was the preceding year of the Tiger; the next Tiger year, twelve years later, would be in 1938.

## CHAPTERS 13–15

In late 1937, the pilots and their wives are given one hour's notice that they must leave Nanking for a distant destination, Kunming in southwest China, taking only one suitcase apiece. Weili gives many of their possessions—clothes, radio, sewing machine—to Wan Betty, the telegraph operator in whom she has found understanding.

The small group traveling together, mostly by truck, consists of Weili and Wen Fu, Hulan and Jiaguo, two other pilots, two officials, an old man, and the truck driver, Old Mr. Ma. The challenging trip of about 1400 miles has five segments:

- From Nanking harbor southwest to the Hankow/Wuchang area via boat on the Yangtze River—about 400 miles on the twisting river, taking several days. (Note: Chiang Kai-shek moves the capital of the Nationalist government to Hankow in December 1937.)
- From Hankow/Wuchang south to Changsha overland by truck, with the passengers crowded together in the back—about 200 miles on narrow dirt roads. Wen Fu shocks everyone by shooting a farmer's stubborn pig that gets in their way.
- From Changsha southwest to Kweiyang—at least 400 miles on dirt roads. While they wait several days for truck repairs and gasoline, they enjoy good food, but must endure a primitive hotel with mattresses infested with stinkbugs and with no enclosed toilet facilities. They learn that Nanking has been cut off by the Japanese.
- From Kweiyang to Heaven's Breath on the mountain ridge—about 200 miles, the last portion of which is a winding, uphill, one-lane road of many switchbacks beginning at a village called Twenty-four Turnarounds. Once they get through the dense fog near the top, they emerge above the clouds and under blue skies to drive along the mountain ridge to the town of Heaven's Breath. Even Wen Fu is moved by the beauty of the summit and breaks into song. In Heaven's Breath, they encounter an army truck on the way to help set up a new seat of government in Chungking. (Note: the transfer of power was completed in October 1938.) They learn that as many as 100,000 people were massacred by the Japanese in Nanking.
- From Heaven's Breath to Kunming—about 200 miles southwest from the mountain ridge.

In summary, the trip from Nanking to Kunming took about two

months, covering approximately 1400 miles of river and primitive roads.

In early 1938, the truck finally reaches Kunming, a crowded, bad-smelling city that serves as a commercial center at the eastern end of the new Burma Road, with Burma itself about 300 miles to the west and French Indochina (later Vietnam) about 150 miles to the south.

After a brief hotel stay, Weili, Hulan, and their husbands move into a two-story house with a third couple, who are heard arguing loudly every night. The man, an inspector of roads, bridges, and railways, soon dies of malaria while checking progress on the construction of the Burma Road. This tragedy allows Weili and Wen Fu to move into better rooms in the house.

In her ninth month of pregnancy, Weili accidentally drops her scissors, which she considers very bad luck. The next day, her first child—a girl—is born dead. She names her Mochou, meaning "sorrowfree," before burying her in nearby foothills that "looked like sleeping maidens."

Over three months later, Weili goes to buy new scissors for the first time and accidentally knocks over a table with forty pairs of scissors. Fleeing home without scissors, she learns that Wen Fu has been seriously injured in an accident while driving an illegally borrowed jeep. He was driving too fast, and a young woman with him was crushed to death under the vehicle. Weili thus learns that Wen Fu has been seeing other women.

After the accident, Wen Fu's erratic violence is heightened to the point of psychotic behavior. Blind in one eye, he makes it impossible for anyone either in the hospital or at home to help with his care, except Weili, and he makes her life increasingly miserable. Hulan convinces Jiaguo not to charge Wen Fu with the crimes of bribery, stealing a jeep, and reckless driving resulting in a death. Although Weili was, in fact, looking forward to Wen Fu's imprisonment, she now feels a traditional indebtedness to Hulan for her intervention, and she performs many favors for Hulan as repayment.

Three pilots visiting Wen Fu witness his unprovoked violence when he knocks their food to the floor and brutally beats a kneeling, begging Weili. She wonders why no one helps her or stands up for her.

Winnie muses about forgiveness as preached by her second husband Jimmy Louie and admits she finds it difficult to replace

# Winnie's Genealogy

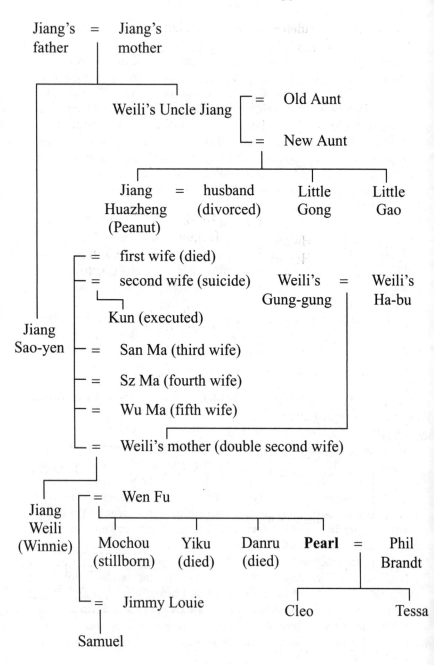

# Helen's Genealogy

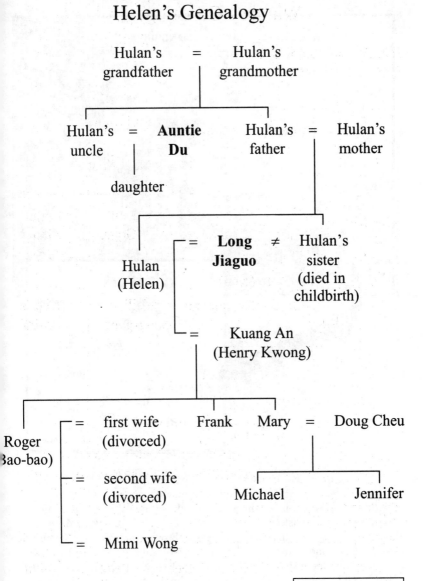

Fearing imminent invasion by the Japanese, Weili and Wen Fu, Hulan and Jiaguo, two other pilots, two officials, an old man, and Old Mr. Ma leave **Nanking** and travel in a ramshackle truck southwest about 400 miles to **Hankow** on the twisting **Yangtze River.** From Hankow, they drive overland on narrow dirt roads to **Changsha.** From Changsha, they continue southwest on more dirt roads. From **Kweiyang**, they travel to **Kunming**, crossing the scenic Heaven's Breath summit. The journey takes about two months and covers about 1400 miles of river and primitive roads.

The **Burma Road** was a dirt road about 800 miles long linking Chungking and Kunming with Lashio, Burma, and, for three years, was the main support line for food and supplies for General Chiang Kai-shek's Nationalist troops.

The war in Asia ended when the U.S. dropped atom bombs on **Hiroshima** and **Nagasaki.**

anger with forgiveness. She compares herself with the unappreciated Kitchen God's wife, whose husband gets all the credit.

In early 1939, Weili has another baby girl—Yiku, "pleasure over bitterness." Wen Fu doesn't come to the hospital for two days, and then arrives with a hangover. He makes the baby cry when he bounces her, and then gets angry at her in a ludicrous confrontation between a day-old infant and an infantile father who claims special treatment as a war hero because he lost sight in one eye in combat. When he doesn't get the food he demands, he goes to the hospital kitchen and demolishes it with a meat cleaver, threatening all the kitchen workers if they report him.

At home, the servant girl asks Weili to let her go, reluctantly revealing that Wen Fu has regularly sexually abused and raped her. Weili sympathizes with the girl and lets her go with extra wages. Weili decides not to confront her husband. ("Don't strike a flea on a tiger's head"—don't settle one trouble only to make a bigger one.)

Several weeks later, Weili learns that the girl has bled to death trying to abort a fetus—Wen Fu's baby. Wen Fu denies Weili's accusations about the girl or any other women and shows no remorse over the girl's death—the second one he has been responsible for. In the storm of his anger, Yiku cries and Wen Fu slaps her several times. From that time on, Yiku exhibits bizarre behavior, especially in the presence of Wen Fu. When a visitor comments on her strange behavior, Wen Fu gets angry and blames Weili for Yiku's actions.

The next day, Yiku has diarrhea and refuses food or drink. Weili runs to the house where the doctor, as well as Wen Fu, is playing mah jong. Wen Fu denies anything is seriously wrong and orders the doctor to stay, admitting, "If she dies, I wouldn't care." Later, Yiku goes into convulsions, and again Weili seeks out the doctor. Wen Fu accuses Weili of not telling them earlier how sick Yiku was. Yiku dies at the hospital.

The quiet end of Yiku's short, chaotic life is portrayed through a final "dialogue" between Weili and Yiku: As Weili watches the life drain out of the child, Yiku's clear eyes seem to absolve Weili—and even Wen Fu: "This is my quick life, no worse, no better than a long one. I accept this, no blame." Acknowledging her own desperation, Weili tells the dead Yiku, "Good for you, little one. You've escaped. Good for you."

Weili is already six or seven months pregnant with her third child.

56

## Commentary

Winnie interrupts her narrative at the beginning of Chapter 13 and at the end of Chapter 14—and periodically throughout her story—to remind Pearl how differently Helen remembers events in which they both participated. The experiences in all three of these chapters illustrate why and how the two women became so closely bonded and yet frequently seem at odds with one another—for example, Weili giving away their possessions, star-gazing and story-telling in the mountains, and sharing the Kunming house and Weili's servants; Hulan persuading Jiaguo not to prosecute Wen Fu, Hulan urging Weili to submit to Wen Fu's humiliating demands, Hulan's false reassurance about Yiku's health, Hulan's delay in getting Yiku to the hospital, and details concerning the deaths of Mochou and Yiku.

For Weili, the extended trip from Nanking to Kunming with new, transitory experiences every day becomes a kind of limbo during which she matures and grows. For instance, having to accommodate severe discomfort and lack of privacy, she becomes less naive and self-conscious. Wen Fu's habitually abusive and contemptuous behavior toward her is virtually suspended during the trip, although the others observe his readiness to violence when he shoots the wandering pig and threatens to shoot the farmer. Weili is even treated to one of his more vulnerable, sympathetic moments when he compares his feelings at the top of the mountains with his experiences while flying. All too quickly after their arrival, however, she is the repeated target of some of his worst behavior.

In these three chapters, Wen Fu exhibits extremes of his erratic behavior which become even more violent and unpredictable after his head injury and loss of sight in one eye, ending his flying career. Wen Fu has always had a strong need for control, probably to compensate for his lack of natural ability. In all aspects of his life—familial, sexual, social, vocational—he must assure himself of some degree of control over others and over his life. When he literally loses control in the jeep accident, his subsequent need for control escalates, making life miserable for those around him whom he thinks he can control—Weili, his daughter Yiku, the nurses, the hospital kitchen employees, and the servant girl.

Wen Fu's rampage in the hospital kitchen, his physical abuse of

Yiku, and his indifference to his responsibility for the deaths of two women suggest a severe mental disorder, perhaps sociopathic, possibly homicidal. In her need to find a reason for his behavior, Weili blames Wen Fu's mother "for letting the meanness in her son grow like a strange appetite, so that he would always feel hungry to feed his own power." The fact that she doesn't blame herself indicates considerable psychological growth for Weili.

Like most Chinese women of her time, Weili initially accepted the traditional roles of men and women, husbands and wives. Wen Fu was the warrior, the wearer of the uniform, the authority, the controller of their lives; Weili was responsible for setting up and keeping house, cooking, sewing, submitting to her husband's sexual demands, bearing and raising children, and even accepting her husband's straying to other women. As her marriage began to deteriorate, though, and her experiences with coping multiplied and became more traumatic, she discovered her inner strengths and identified her own needs, adapting her role for greater self-development and independence.

---

- *mu*   approximately eight-tenths of an acre.

- *dan-dan* **noodles**   Szechuan noodles served in a peppery sauce.

- **patterns of gods and goddesses of the night sky**   patterns of stars that form constellations, often named after mythical characters.

- **Yunnanese**   natives of Yunnan province, a perennially disputed border territory in southwest China adjoining Myanmar, Laos, and Vietnam (formerly Burma, Siam, and French Indochina). Kunming is Yunnan's capital.

- **the Burma Road**   a dirt road about eight hundred miles long, completed in January 1939 to link Kunming with Lashio, Burma—the lifeline that supplied General Chiang Kai-shek's troops for three years. Freighter shipments entered Rangoon, on Burma's southern coast, and traveled 350 miles north by rail to Lashio, from where they were trucked to Kunming. Burma was under British control at this time.

- **malaria ate up his brain**   Malaria is a disease dating to ancient times in Asia. Parasites introduced into the bloodstream by the bite of a disease-carrying mosquito afflict major organs—kidneys, spleen, and brain—sometimes causing blackwater fever, coma, and death.

- **characters were written one on top of another**   Before twentieth-century simplification, Chinese characters, called graphemes or pictograms, were combined with other graphemes to create abstract concepts. For example, the symbol for *mother* was topped by the symbol for *mouth* to create the verb *scold*, a verb that would be difficult to draw without symbolic linkage to concrete nouns. This semantic notation via word clusters or radicals resulted in 50,000 characters, as demonstrated by an eighteenth-century Chinese dictionary. The burden of so much complex memory work deprived many Chinese of literacy. Only the wealthy had the money and leisure to be tutored in the entire Chinese vocabulary. Today, more people can learn Chinese because the character base has been pared down to two thousand units.

- **Double Seventh**   the forty-ninth day after the Chinese New Year; because 49 is the square of seven, it is generally considered a magic number. (Note: Winnie received her kitchenware and silver chopsticks on the seventh day of trousseau shopping, a suggestion that food, cooking, and the chopsticks would bring her good fortune.)

- **Mr. Roosevelt, Mr. Churchill**   The reference is to Franklin Delano Roosevelt (president of the United States) and Sir Winston Churchill (prime minister of England). The United States and England were both helping the Chinese defend themselves against their Japanese aggressors.

- **night soil**   human waste that is collected and used as fertilizer by some. Weili thinks Yiku's illness may come from vegetables Hulan bought from the Burmese, who used human waste as fertilizer, which could have spread germs causing cholera, dysentery, and typhoid fever.

- **Buddha**   Usually pictured in a tranquil seated pose, the Buddha represents the contemplative life of the "enlightened one," Siddhartha Gautama (563–483 B.C.), who conceived a faith based on asceticism or self-denial that leads to nirvana—a simple, elusive paradise resulting from obliteration of self.

## CHAPTERS 16 & 17

From her son Danru's first day of life in 1940, Weili is determined that he not be like Wen Fu, even if he resembles Wen Fu in some features. Wen Fu is now being trained in radio communications, since he can no longer fly.

When Weili returns home after Danru's birth, she finds not only that Hulan's widowed Auntie Du Ching has moved into the house from northern China, but also that Wen Fu has moved a beautiful, illiterate young woman, Min, into her bed. Actually pleased that Wen Fu has someone to meet his sexual needs, Weili simply moves the concubine into another room and lets Wen Fu go to her regularly. Weili finds Min to be good company, and they become friends, even as Wen Fu begins to tire of her. Formerly a dancer and singer in a Shanghai club called The Great World, Min learns from Weili how to be more ladylike and how to write her name; in turn, she teaches Weili the tango and other dances.

Auntie Du finally tells Weili what she already knows—that Wen Fu has been fooling around with Min—and something she does not know—that Min is pregnant. Weili decides to use this nominal disgrace as an excuse to divorce Wen Fu and take Danru away. Wen Fu, however, tears up the divorce paper she prepares.

Min leaves the house and Weili tracks her down to give her money for an abortion. Min has already had an abortion, but Weili gives her money anyway. Min leaves town, and Weili compares her own life with the bizarre illusion of torture that Min once performed at The Great World.

The following summer, in 1941, Weili still reassures herself Danru is not like Wen Fu. Meanwhile her life with Wen Fu continues to deteriorate, as does China's existence after the closing of the Burma Road by the British, who were absorbed in the fight against their German enemies nearer home. Jiaguo and Wen Fu go to Chungking for a while to train military personnel for defense and to set up an early warning system. Weili determines that if she can't change her fate, she must change her attitude.

Weili is finally so upset by Hulan's poor vision that she takes her for glasses, and Hulan is amazed at what she can see with glasses. Just then, Weili, Hulan, and Danru are caught in a devastating Japanese air raid of Kunming, the first of many.

Weili helps Hulan read part of a letter from Jiaguo and learns that Jiaguo and Hulan have had a sexless marriage, an issue they argued about just before he left. Hulan does not realize Weili read that part of the letter and continues to keep the matter a secret.

In another destructive air raid, Weili, Hulan, and Danru are separated, but they all survive safely.

## Commentary

Interaction with the two new women of the house intensifies

Weili's reliance on sisterhood—a reassuring wartime interdependence among female noncombatants to help each other cope with the servility and powerlessness imposed by patriarchy, as well as with the terrors of bombardment. Auntie Du, the sage adviser, nudges Weili out of her naiveté toward self-preservation, especially in the matters of Min's pregnancy and Wen Fu's growing disaffection with Weili and their marriage.

Divorce, an unthinkable alternative in early twentieth-century China, nevertheless becomes a necessity in Weili's mind. In her first attempt, she plans to get Wen Fu to agree to a divorce so he can have Min, and then she and Danru will sail from Haiphong to her father's house in Shanghai. Her plan fails because she doesn't acknowledge Wen Fu's need for control. His show of mastery of his wife leads to divorce papers as tattered and worthless as Weili's self-esteem. His swagger carries the moment with its ill-concealed malice: "When I want to divorce you, I will tell you. You don't tell me what to do."

For the second time, Weili envies someone who has escaped from Wen Fu's manipulation and bullying. She takes comfort in Danru's obedience and trust, and her thoughts as she contemplates Danru's future exemplify the **internal monologue** that echos through her mind:

- the urge to flee pain and fear
- a maternal instinct calling for gentle, uplifting words to her children
- a need for peace through placation of an insane husband
- an acquiescence to the parade of nameless, faceless paramours whom Wen Fu frequents
- a tenuous tolerance of the game of one-upmanship that Wen Fu perpetrates on his resilient wife
- the instinctual will to survive.

A unifying thread of Amy Tan's novel is the verbalization of snippets of logic, self-assurance, and self-preservation that Weili whispers to herself from the 1930s right up to the unburdening of her spirit to Pearl after Auntie Du's funeral in 1990. While observing tribal groups at Han rallies, Weili remembers a common Chinese saying that typifies her current coping style: "If you can't change your fate, change your attitude," an expression comparable to the American truism, "If life gives you lemons, make lemonade."

After four years of making assumptions about Hulan's marriage and her comments about Weili's marriage, Weili accidentally learns that the facts of Hulan's marriage are quite different. Unknown to Hulan, Weili reads part of a letter from Jiaguo promising that he will return in the spring and assume the role of a proper husband—that is, he will assume his sexual responsibilities toward Hulan. Weili suddenly understands Hulan's position. Hulan lives with a guilt-ridden man who withholds sex from the sister of a woman whose death he caused. Weili, who smarts at Hulan's betrayals after Wen Fu's insane attacks and crazed sexual assaults, realizes that Hulan would trade a sexless union for the fulfillment of regular marital relations and a child like Danru. Each wife envies the other for the perceived wholeness of the other's marriage.

---

- **Ginger Rogers and Fred Astaire movie pictures** Hollywood's famous dancing duo who started out separately as child dancer/actors, then teamed up in ten popular movies for RKO Studio during the 1930s, including *Top Hat* (1935) and *Swing Time* (1936).

- **tango, fox-trot, lindy hop** contrasting dance styles. The first is a smooth, sensuous Latin dance that requires intense coordination of long, gliding steps, interlocking gaze, and intertwining legs. In contrast, the fox-trot is a rather tame, but safe choice of dance steps, variations on the box step to a brisk 4/4 beat. The lindy hop, a vigorous dance named in honor of flier Charles A. Lindbergh, contrasts the tango and fox-trot with its energetic rhythm and gymnastic steps.

- **cholera epidemic** a common result of hasty refugee camps and contaminated water and food. A fast-moving killer, cholera depletes the body of electrolytes as a result of diarrhea and vomiting. The human wastes, loaded with bacilli, spread the disease by contaminating linens, groundwater, hands of patients and health workers, and food supplies.

- **Han blood** A distinct, proud Oriental race, the Han or Han-Jen, whose ties with a ruling family date to 202 B. C., predominate in north central, northeastern, eastern, and southeastern China.

- **kaoliang cakes** hard, dried patties made from meal mixed with either pumpkin or turnip, topped with sausage, and eaten cold or fried as a New Year's delicacy.

## CHAPTERS 18 & 19

The time is Christmas 1941, and the Americans at the Kunming air base sponsor a victory dance to celebrate the success of the Flying Tigers. Weili meets and dances with a tall, handsome, good-humored Asian-American. The healthy open joy and the wholesome sexuality in Jimmy Louie's smiles strike Weili at the right moment in her maturity. To herself, she admits that, at age twenty-two, she is ripe to "be caught by happiness, like a fish in a net."

Jimmy is a translator with the United States Information Service. Women flock to him for easily pronounced, Americanized versions of their Chinese names. Among those he finds names for are Hulan (whom he names Helen), Weili (whom he names Winnie), and their husbands—Jock for Jiaguo, and Victor for Wen Fu. Predictably, Wen Fu demands something more special than his wife's name and more unusual than all others. Jimmy Louie then suggests Judas as Wen Fu's new name, "someone who changed history forever." Wen Fu likes the power connotation, not knowing about Judas of the Christian New Testament, but Weili does and is secretly delighted. She and Jimmy share their private joke on Wen Fu during a romantic dance to "Moonlight Serenade."

Jimmy Louie's effect on Weili does not escape Wen Fu's attention. After the dance, Wen Fu calls her abusive names for dancing with Jimmy, and he threatens to divorce her. To her secret joy, she writes out the divorce statement he demands. Then he threatens to take Danru, forces her to beg for his forgiveness, and finally rapes her at gunpoint, humiliating her every way he knows.

After he leaves for work the next morning, Weili packs a few clothes and takes the discarded divorce paper, hoping that Hulan and Auntie Du will be the needed witnesses on the paper. Hulan refuses to believe that Wen Fu is a monster, rejoicing that there were no witnesses to the signing of the divorce papers. Sanguine and cheerful, she urges, "Now sit down, eat your morning meal. Calm down, no more worries." They will not be witnesses for her, but they finally agree to help her get away and find a place to stay until Hulan finds transportation out of the area.

Weili and Danru take refuge in a filthy rooming house nearby. They are awakened the next morning by Wen Fu's roaring voice. Thinking Wen Fu will be remorseful and kind once he knows how upset Weili is, Hulan has told him where to find them. Instead, over the months that follow, he continues his abuse of Weili. She repeatedly becomes pregnant and repeatedly has abortions because she wants no more of his babies. She considers suicide many times, but cannot bring herself to carry it out. This bitter low of Weili's life continues for more than three years at Kunming.

The war begins to turn in China's favor as the armies (with help from the Allies) gradually push back the Japanese. This gives new life to the internal power struggle between the Chinese Nationalists and the Chinese Communists. Finally, in August 1945, the families learn that the Japanese have gone forever. (What Weili does not mention is that the Americans dropped atom bombs on Hiroshima and Nagasaki, and the Japanese surrendered to the Allies.) After a seven-year absence from Shanghai and an eight-year marriage to a child and wife batterer, Weili looks forward to an immediate return to the protection of her father.

In sisterly fashion, Hulan and Weili exchange gifts and, with their families, separate at Wuchang—Weili, Wen Fu, and Danru to Shanghai—Hulan, Jiaguo, and Auntie Du to Harbin in the far northeast.

In September, nearing her father's home, Weili sorts through the perversities of her life with Wen Fu and prepares to tell her father about the untenable pattern of abuse. However, his severe physical and mental debilitation prevents Weili from confiding in him, and Wen Fu's Kuomintang uniform strikes fear into the old man. San Ma, Weili's honorary mother, tells Weili the details of slanderous newspaper articles about Jiang, the unexpected resurgence of his five factories under Japanese management, his personal dishonor, and the stroke that has left him partially paralyzed and mute. According to San Ma, Jiang's helpless physical state saves him from a traitor's execution by the Kuomintang, but not from the spite of local patriots. Wen Fu's family soon install themselves in the house and begin selling off Jiang's priceless antiques, quickly running through most of what is left of the Jiang family wealth.

## Commentary

As the **denouement**, or **falling action**, of the novel begins, Jimmy Louie appears almost as though he were the **deus ex machina**, the hero waiting in the wings ever since Winnie first began confessing past hurts and fears to Pearl. An unlikely rescuer, Jimmy brings to Weili what has been missing from her personal life—the supportive relationship of a man who begins his courtship with simple acts of friendship, building Weili's trust into a lifelong love.

Like her incessant search for bargains, Weili has been cheated out of the best of men. Change from the past will require significant character development. Still chained to the evil, swaggering, self-absorbed Wen Fu, she must assert total independence, find a way to escape with Danru, and accept Jimmy Louie as her lover in much the same way that her mother may have deserted her own marriage. The promise of a daring escape as prelude to a normal life entices Weili to take chances that bring out a survivalist streak in her character as yet unseen in the novel and unknown to Pearl.

At this point, the novel moves full circle on symbolic feet: Peanut had lured Wen Fu during Chinese New Year by hobbling herself in a tight-bottomed coat and tottering on ridiculous high heels through the marketplace in a display of inappropriate fashion. Weili, whose ill fortune placed her in Peanut's stead as Wen Fu's wife, breaks the curse of his mounting savagery, child abuse, and tirades while struggling to cope with a broken heel of a shoe at the Christmas dance. Amid decorations carried at great risk over the Burma Road, Weili breaks her heel, takes a personal risk at bettering her life, and is rescued by a man who falls in love with her. Jimmy Louie makes a lifetime joke out of it: "I fell in love with her right from the beginning. As for Winnie—she only fell. But what matters is I caught her." (Note the parallel here to the fainting episode in Chapter 3, when onetime-suitor Dr. Lin diagnoses heat stroke and Jimmy Louie carries his wife into the church to get her out of the sun. She recalls that Jimmy "had once baptized me to save my soul. And now, he said, both laughing and crying, the doctor had baptized me to save my life.")

The treachery that follows Weili's pleasant evening at the dance and the subsequent abuse at gunpoint weaken the sisterhood rituals that have united her with Hulan. After Hulan betrays her by leading Wen Fu to her hideaway, Weili nurtures a bitterness that still taints their friendship in 1990. Although Hulan will eventually become convinced of Wen Fu's psychopathic behavior and of Weili's suffering—and will even declare she knew about them all along—Weili continues to endure humiliating sexual episodes with a man who uses her "as if I were—what?—a machine!" Weili aborts the fetuses of the next three pregnancies to save more children from abuse. In frustration at her virtual enslavement, she recalls, "I cried to myself, This is a sin—to give a baby such a bad life! . . . So I let those other babies die. In my heart, I was being kind." Tan justifies Weili's drastic actions—consistent with today's pro-choice position—on the rationale of avoiding future violence to their children. In 1990, Winnie looks to Pearl as a woman who can empathize with so deep a depression that the young Weili wanted to die.

Balancing the despair of Wen Fu's recapture of Weili and Danru are the joyous cries of national victory and the sweet-sad ritual that requires an exchange of gifts to mark the separation of wartime friends. Auntie Du, lacking an item of worth to give Weili, laments that she will receive a treasured perfume bottle, but that Weili must travel on to Shanghai empty-handed. Weili's gentle thanks for a surrogate mother and grandmother for Danru smooth over the embarrassment. Weili apologizes to Hulan at the last minute for having disputed Hulan's report of how many beans she should pick up with chopsticks without dropping any. In a departing gesture of love, Hulan offers a rare commodity in Chinese social intercourse: She tells Weili the truth about a depth of poverty that required her to count out individual beans to share with her sister for their daily nourishment.

---

- **Macy's**   a large American department store chain.

- **ah-vuh-gee**   a phonetic pronunciation of the initials of the American Volunteer Group.

- **"Air Mail Special"**   a wartime song hit composed in 1941 by Big Band leader Benny Goodman.

- **"Moonlight Serenade"**   One of the romantic hits of the Big Band era, this song was written by Mitchell Parish and Glenn Miller in 1939 and became the memorable theme song of Glenn Miller's orchestra.

- **stinky bean curd**   a fermented bean paste or purée baked like brie and served soft and runny as a breakfast food.

- **phoenix**   a fictional bird from ancient eastern Mediterranean lore. The one-of-a-kind phoenix lives its five-hundred-year life span, then climbs onto a funeral pyre and sets itself aflame. From its ashes springs a worm that develops into a new phoenix decked in radiant red, purple, and gold plumage.

- **Imperial Emperor Hirohito**   Japan's titular leader during World War II. Hirohito (1901–1989), who was revered like a god, actually had little power over military incursions in Manchuria and the Hawaiian Islands, yet insisted on a surrender, which he delivered over national radio in an uncharacteristic person-to-person communication with his subjects. At the end of the war, the Allies stripped Hirohito of all but ceremonial significance and left Japan's governance to its parliament.

- **Wen Tai-tai**   a respectful title indicating that Wen Fu's mother is assuming the position of lady of the house in Jiang's residence.

- **fen**   1/100 of a Chinese penny.

## CHAPTERS 20–23

In early 1946, Weili is again determined to run away from her marriage, taking Danru with her, even if it means poverty for them. Before she leaves, she wants to visit her aunts on Tsungming Island. After she and Danru both recover from jaundice acquired on their trip from Kunming to Shanghai, she takes him to visit the aunts. They are kind and welcoming amidst their own disappointments and losses. Wieli learns that Peanut, a Communist now, ran away from her own marriage and was divorced by her husband. Each of the aunts secretly gives Weili Peanut's address in Shanghai.

Back home after her two weeks on Tsungming Island, Weili secretly goes to visit Peanut, who is now living in a dirty and crowded section of Shanghai. Along the street near Peanut's house, she accidentally encounters Jimmy Louie, whom she has not seen since the Christmas dance in 1941. He insists, "We loved each other from the moment we met, that's why our two wills joined together to find each other." Over tea, he restates his love and she tells him "how everything has changed, but nothing has become better" for her. She confides in him about the unfortunate circumstances of her entire family and about her intention to find Peanut, but she says little about Wen Fu. Jimmy is still unmarried, although he carries a picture of four young women in one family, any of whom would make a good wife for him. They talk so long, it becomes too late for her to meet Peanut. They agree to meet again the following morning before she visits Peanut. Jimmy leaves the picture of the four women on the table.

The next day, everything seems to conspire against her getting away for the rendezvous, but she finally arrives at their meeting place an hour and a half late. She is overwhelmed with joy to find him still waiting for her.

Weili finally tells Jimmy about Wen Fu and that she is visiting Peanut to find out more about getting a divorce. Jimmy walks with her to Peanut's house and says he will wait for her to talk with Peanut, regardless of how long it takes.

Peanut is pleased to see her. Not only is she a Communist activist, but she and the mother of a girl they both knew (Little Yu) operate this house as a way station for women running from their marriages. Peanut tells about her own marriage to a man who was homosexual and may have been a hermaphrodite—a person with both male and female genitals. The man's family did not want her to divorce him, so she ran away, and eventually he divorced her.

Weili eats a meal with Peanut, Little Yu's mother, and several other women in their house. She hears their stories and they hear hers. Peanut urges her to take all the money and jewelry she can when she leaves home.

Jimmy is still waiting for her outside Peanut's, and she announces to him that she will run away from Wen Fu with Danru. They work out a signal by telephone after which Jimmy will meet her and take her to Peanut's house temporarily.

Back at her father's house, Weili worries about what will happen to her father after she leaves. Although she has little hope he will understand, she tells him secretly that she is running away and doesn't expect his forgiveness. His reaction first appears angry but is in fact an attempt to show her where he has hidden three small gold ingots in the bottom rod of the scroll painting he had damaged when the Japanese came to him. Astounded, she accepts the gold, but hides it temporarily in the rod.

The next morning, she tells the family that Old Aunt is very sick and she needs to go to Tsungming Island again. San Ma encourages her (probably realizing what is happening), but no one else seems to care. The next morning, she takes a small suitcase into which she puts the gold pieces and leaves the house with Danru.

Much of Chapter 23 is narrated as though Winnie were showing Pearl a photograph album of pictures taken by Jimmy during the period that followed her escape from Wen Fu. Weili and Danru first go to Peanut's house, where Little Yu's mother tries to send her and Danru away from Shanghai and Wen Fu. Jimmy objects, and instead they go to live with him, remaining in Shanghai. For several months, they are all very happy and virtually carefree. In the meantime, Peanut informs the aunts that Weili is living with another man, and the news eventually reaches Wen Fu. Meanwhile, he is turning more and more of Jiang Sao-yen's money and possessions into worthless "new money." With the last of her dowry, Weili hires a lawyer to arrange for the divorce. The lawyer's office is vandalized and the divorce paper signed by Wen Fu is destroyed, apparently by Wen Fu's henchmen. Weili and Jimmy decide to send Danru north to Harbin to be with Hulan and Auntie Du, out of the reach of Wen Fu.

On one of the most tragic days of her life, Weili is visited by Auntie Du, who tells her that Danru has died in an epidemic which also claimed Jiaguo.

Weili is unexpectedly arrested and sent to a women's prison for stealing her husband's son and letting him die, for stealing valuables from her husband's family, and for deserting her husband. Wen Fu, it is said, has filled the ears of the authorities, including the American consul, with lies and half-truths. Without the divorce papers she claims Wen Fu signed, the judge sentences her to two years in prison, unless she goes back to Wen Fu. She chooses prison.

Auntie Du brings her basic clothing, a few personal items, and the newspaper with headlines about her now infamous love affair with an American soldier. The story built from Wen Fu's lies soon results in Jimmy's being asked to leave China. He promises to return for her in two years.

Although the prison cells are primitive, Weili not only learns to survive, but she helps make life better for other women prisoners. She teaches some of them to read and write, she shows them ways to speak and act properly, and she introduces them to ways to keep themselves and their quarters neater and cleaner. Both guards and prisoners become her friends and confidantes. She learns that Min has committed suicide, that Peanut and Little Yu's mother have been forced to leave Shanghai, and finally that her father has died, after he made a final conscious effort to mislead Wen Fu into thinking that gold was hidden in the house walls. San Ma and Wu Ma are leaving the family house to live in Wu Ma's brother's home. The final memento in the album is the telegram Weili sent to Jimmy in the U.S., asking if she can come to America to be his wife.

## Commentary

These four chapters exemplify Weili's emergence as a strong, self-motivated woman, unique for her generation and time. From her determination to end her marriage to Wen Fu, to her kind, quiet authority in improving the quality of prison life and the individual lives of several prisoners, Weili reveals the self-assurance and unflinching motivation which have surfaced and now empower the uncertain, naive girl abandoned by her mother long ago and thrown into the role of feudal wife to a psychotic man.

The group of women in transition at Peanut's house both challenge and support Weili's determination. One of them reminds her, for example, that giving up old forms of pride may free her from misery. Her acceptance of this special group's logic helps not only in her flight from Wen Fu, but in her move toward Jimmy Louie. From that afternoon on, Weili and Jimmy become "two people talking with one heart."

Jimmy Louie has perceived Weili's hidden strengths from the beginning, referring to her as a woman "who could do anything; dance with broken shoes or in your bare feet. Fragile-looking, yet strong and brave, the kind of person nothing could stop." To Jimmy Louie, Weili's strength is the pragmatic sort—the assessment of what is possible and what is too costly for her spirit to survive. Putting his adoration into moral support, Jimmy Louie enables her to view herself as a winner, a term echoed by the nickname, Winnie, he gave her in 1941 (and, ironically, by the name Victor offered to Wen Fu, but which Wen Fu spurned as not good enough). To be a winner, Weili must negotiate with reality, make hard choices, and abandon valued portions of the past, notably the last days of Jiang's life and her home in Shanghai.

Having looked for escape with the help of Hulan and Auntie Du, her father, her aunts, Peanut, and even Jimmy Louie, the focal issue becomes clear: Weili must rely on her own inner strengths and stop looking for outside rescue from her failed marriage.

Throughout the novel, Tan has used minor characters to play critical parts, like cameo players in films. In these chapters, for example, Little Yu's mother plays a significant role in Weili's plans. In Chapter 16, the concubine Min becomes an early focus for Weili's kindness, teaching, and even admiration, and in the current chapters, the report of Min's death helps Weili realize that her own strength may be greater than what she perceived in Min.

Weili experiences the extremes of emotion in short order: from joy with Jimmy and Danru, to despair and guilt over Danru's death away from her, followed soon by a chain of miseries—her arrest, her unjust trial and public humiliation, her imprisonment, and the banishment of Jimmy from China. The judge states the ultimate in feudal justice: "a husband has the right to sue a wife for taking his property and his son." Pronounced guilty by the court, Weili has her own little ironic victory when she chooses two years in prison over "freedom" under the tyranny of her abusive husband.

The **motif** of material resources is a significant adjunct to the story of Chinese women, who pass from feudalism to nationalism to Japanese colonialism to communism with little change in their social status. On Weili's arrival at Tsungming Island, for example, while Old Aunt and New Aunt beam at their niece, Weili witnesses the sad spectacle of an older generation worn down by the perils and hardships of Japanese occupation.

Ironically, part of Weili's ability to withstand the war and make her own way derives from a holdover from patriarchal times—her dowry, the money that Jiang deposits in a Shanghai bank for her personal use. She alone controls her dowry, although some of it falls into Wen Fu's hands and disappears over the gambling table or for buying a jalopy, while Weili uses much of it to lessen their wartime privations. By New Year 1945, Weili has drawn heavily against the four thousand yuan over the eight years of her marriage. The wartime economy reduces the surviving sum to a few hundred American dollars in value. After moving in with Jimmy Louie, Weili is glad that his salary is in American dollars rather than Chinese currency and that her jewelry and few valuable possessions can be converted into liquid assets, a more trustworthy form of empowerment than reliance on relatives, superstition, lovers, or governments.

A strong **dramatic irony** springs from the pantomimed defiance of Jiang Sao-yen. When suborned by materialistic Japanese officials who finger his antiques and urge him to comply with the Emperor Hirohito as an example to other Chinese patriots, Jiang replies—prophetically without words—by tossing tea on the representation of spring in a valuable four-part scroll series, three of which Wen Fu later sells. After a stroke afflicts Jiang with the inability to speak, he communicates through gestures. He acknowledges the intent of his defiant daughter to run away by opening the rod of the damaged scroll and handing her his cache of gold. Approving of her actions but unable to verbalize his thoughts, he has observed Wen Fu's Machiavellian behavior and makes no effort to overrule Weili's decision to flee a lawful feudal marriage. Reaching back into the spring scene, Weili conceals the three small ingots once more until her plans are complete. Like spring buds themselves, the ingots lie in their protective covering until the time is right for Weili's blossoming. Finally, even at the very end of his life, her father's defiance plays one final joke that causes Wen Fu to start tearing the house apart looking for non-existent gold in the walls.

---

- **opium**  a milky white addictive substance extracted from the unripe seed pod of the poppy. A folk remedy and anesthetic from ancient times, pure opium is so hazardous to health that China attempted to exterminate the profitable opium trade in the eighteenth century, when demand for the drug spread to Europe.

- **river crabs**  The refugees' contraction of jaundice, a symptom of liver malfunction, suggests a potentially virulent type of schistosomiasis or bilharziasis caused by a common water-borne parasite that invades the liver, spreading infection, diminishing the organ's ability to cleanse the blood of impurities, and often resulting in death.

- **ginseng root**  the major, costly palliative of Chinese herbal pharmacopoeia, which for a thousand years has been revered as a tonic to increase mental and physical capacities and to curb the loss of faculties in old age.

- **rope lattice frames**  Chinese beds utilize hemp rope as cheap, adjustable bedsprings. As the hemp stretches, it is tightened or replaced with stronger material to hold the mattress level.

- **American Consulate General**  the jurisdiction of American authority in mutual American-Chinese affairs. After World War II, the office was governed by an appointed ambassador who spoke for U. S. President Harry S. Truman.

- **bittermelon**  a round, green, seed-filled member of the squash family that resembles a sweet melon and is dried and served like a vegetable, usually as an accompaniment to beef. To Weili and the other runaway wives, the melon symbolizes the bitterness they must swallow as a part of an unhappy life.

**CHAPTERS 24–26**

A remarried and pregnant Hulan visits Weili in prison in February 1949. Hulan has asked her new husband, Kuang An, to use his government connections to get Weili released. Two months later, the prison officials free her with no questions, no explanation, except that the document she must sign says "court error." With Auntie Du, who has come to prison to meet her, she returns to the apartment where she, Jimmy, and Danru had lived, and where Hulan, her husband, and Auntie Du now live.

Weili is profuse in her thanks to Kuang. She learns only later from Auntie Du that it wasn't he who obtained her release. Auntie Du herself had won Weili's freedom by telling the authorities that Weili was related to one of the high-ranking Communists about to take over Shanghai. (Hulan never finds out that her husband was not the one who got Weili out of prison.)

Weili sends a telegram to Jimmy in the U.S., and he invites her to come immediately to California as his wife. Weili gets a visa and tickets for three different routes out of China. To get Wen Fu to sign divorce papers again, Weili tricks him and his current "wife" into picking up a package needing signatures of both him and his wife. Before he can possess what he will later discover is a box of donkey dung, he must sign the papers acknowledging that he and Weili were divorced in 1941.

Within days, Wen Fu stalks Weili to her apartment, rapes her at gunpoint, tears up the divorce papers, and takes the tickets, but before he can leave, Hulan interrupts them. Between Weili and Hulan, they force him to remove his trousers, they retrieve the tickets, and they throw his trousers out the window to the street. As he chases after them, he vows Weili will never be through with him.

The next day, Weili is on a plane to California and six days later with Jimmy Louie. Five days after that, the Communists occupy Shanghai—and no one can leave.

About nine months later—maybe a little less—Pearl is born.

In Chapter 25, the narration returns to Pearl's point of view in the present tense, and she suddenly realizes that the terrible Wen Fu may have been her father, although Winnie is not direct about it here.

Pearl then tells her mother about her multiple sclerosis. Although Winnie is furious that Pearl should have to suffer such a disease—perhaps a legacy of Wen Fu, Winnie says—Pearl feels hopeful about herself, now that her mother knows.

At Bao-bao's reception, Helen tells Pearl that all three of them—Winnie, Helen, and Pearl—should take a trip to China to obtain Chinese remedies to overcome Pearl's MS.

Chapter 26, the last chapter in the novel, is told in Winnie's voice in current time. Helen admits to Winnie that she knew all along that Wen Fu was a "bad man" and that she knew Winnie was worried Wen Fu might be Pearl's father.

Winnie goes to buy a replacement for the Kitchen God's picture in the little altar—hoping to find a god, perhaps as yet unknown, something more representative of hope and healing. The shop owner sells her an unmarked porcelain statue of a woman seated comfortably in her chair. This female statue will replace the Kitchen God, but she will not be called Mrs. Kitchen God; there will be no reference any more to the cruel Kitchen God.

Winnie paints a name for the goddess in gold on the bottom. Pearl first sees it when Winnie is offering her some herbal Chinese remedies, and she cries when she realizes it is for her. Winnie tells Pearl that she can talk to the goddess and confide in her: "She will listen. She will wash away everything sad with her tears. She will use her stick to chase away everything bad. See her name: Lady Sorrow-free, happiness winning over bitterness, no regrets in this world."

## Commentary

As the novel comes to a quick close in these three chapters, it helps to put these events against the backdrop of ups and downs in Weili's life and well-being:

- *down* as a six-year-old girl abandoned by her mother, sent away by her father, and largely ignored by her uncle and aunts who assume responsibility for her upbringing
- *up* as the bride of an admired pilot and imminent war hero
- *down* as she experiences Wen Fu's pleasure in her humiliation and abuse
- *up* as she makes friends who recognize her strengths
- *down* as Wen Fu brings new shame and betrayals into her life
- *up* as she has her children
- *down* as three of them are taken from her
- *up* as Hulan agrees to help her escape

- *down* as Hulan betrays her by divulging her hiding place to Wen Fu
- *up* as she meets Jimmy Louie and later meets him again and plans escape with him
- *down* as she is arrested, brought to trial on half-truths and lies, and finally imprisoned
- *up* when she adjusts to her prison life, and when she is released before her two years are complete, and when Jimmy asks her to come immediately to the U.S. as his wife
- *down* as Wen Fu takes revenge on her trick at the telegraph office by raping her at gunpoint and threatening her emigration
- *up* when she terrorizes him with his own gun and strips him of his pants, and when she gets on the plane to the United States and Jimmy Louie
- *down* when she worries that Wen Fu's rape may have resulted not only in the conception of her only living daughter, but also in Pearl's life-threatening illness
- and finally *up* when she achieves a new level of trust and openness with Pearl, capped by the replacement of the Kitchen God with a goddess: Lady Sorrowfree.

Utilizing skillful control of character and motivation and a return to **framework narrative**, Tan maintains **suspense** and continues **character development** well into the last three chapters. Here are significant revelations about:

- how Weili is actually released from prison and becomes indebted to Hulan's Auntie Du
- the final humiliation of Weili and her modest vengeance on Wen Fu
- how Weili escapes from China
- why there is a question about Pearl's father
- how Pearl finally tells her mother about her multiple sclerosis
- how the emotional distance between Pearl and her mother is bridged
- how Helen has been using a non-existent brain tumor to get sympathy and to press for the sharing of secrets.

The longtime, apparently indestructible friendship between Winnie and Helen still thrives on secrets, as well as on their frequent arguments (usually trivial). Continuing secrets, for example, include: Winnie has never told Helen that it was Auntie Du and not Henry Kwong who got her released from prison; Helen wants Winnie to continue thinking Helen has a brain tumor, so she will go with her to China for herbal remedies. Typical arguments in these final chapters include: Winnie's firm refusal of the last scallop offered her by Helen, their differing views of the expense of traveling to China, and why the tea they had in Hangchow was so sweet.

The end of Winnie's story and Pearl's immediate reactions leave a nagging uncertainty which will persist for both Winnie and Pearl: Was Pearl's biological father the despised Wen Fu or the beloved Jimmy Louie? In Chapter 4, Winnie says, "Wen Fu, that bad man, he was Pearl's father." Yet in Chapter 25, after Pearl asks, "Who are you saying was my father?" Winnie rushes to reassure her:

> Daddy [Jimmy Louie] was your *father*. . . . Of course. I would never let that bad man claim you for his daughter. He would never have that from me. . . . Oh, I know what you are thinking. Of course, every baby is born with *yin* and *yang*. The *yin* comes from the woman. The *yang* comes from the man. When you were born I tried to see whose *yang* you had. I tried to see your daddy. I would say, Look she has Jimmy Louie's smile. I tried to forget everything else. But inside my heart I saw something else. . . . You looked like Mochou. You looked like Yiku. You looked like Danru, Danru especially. All of them together. All the children I could not keep but could never forget.

Winnie seems ambivalent, even as she tries to convince Pearl. Her actions and thoughts in the closing scenes show her still growing and coping with difficult and unforeseen circumstances in her life—perhaps her fate: For example, an assertive, unvanquished Winnie displaces her grief over Pearl's Wen-like *yang* with new worries about MS, which she sees as an untouchable evil stalking Pearl. In another example, Winnie rips up and burns the grinning Kitchen God—Wen Fu's deified double—and sets out on a quest for a nebulous female quality, an unnamed strength to quell all the smirking Wen Fus who ever neglected, terrorized, and killed their children or intimidated, stalked, and raped women.

To Mrs. Hong, the proprietor's wife at Sam Fook's Trading Company, Winnie admits, "I am looking for a goddess that nobody knows. Maybe she does not yet exist." Winnie purchases a fallible goddess, one that the factory has forgotten to identify. The qualities of the smiling statue are traits that Winnie embraces for herself and for Pearl: comfortable-looking, unworried, wise, innocent, understanding. With her own hand, Winnie inscribes a name on her personal goddess. She is a blend of Mochou and Pearl, Winnie and Helen, Auntie Du and the women in the Shanghai prison and in Peanut's way station for runaway wives. The embodiment of hope and female empowerment, she could only be Lady Sorrowfree.

---

- **lox and bagels**   a popular breakfast combination or snack food, traditionally considered Jewish-American in origin, consisting of paper thin slices of smoked salmon and a doughnut-shaped roll, often spread with cream cheese and served with pungent capers and fresh onion slices.

- **oy vay**   a Yiddish expression of dismay.

- **costume from *Les Misèrables***   In the original production of the musical based on Victor Hugo's novel, one memorable dress was made of layers of irregular-shaped pieces of filmy fabric, hanging in tatters around the girl's legs.

# CRITICAL ESSAYS

## CHARACTER ANALYSIS: JIANG WEILI/WINNIE LOUIE

Clearly the character Jiang Weili—later Winnie Louie—has the primary responsibility for carrying the story, for keeping the reader involved and for making the novel believable. To the reader, she becomes a real person with many commendable qualities, but she is not perfect. How does this woman of another time and another place become so real, so admirable, so familiar, and yet we are always learning something new about her, right to the last page? We may find answers by studying not Weili's primary experiences in the novel, but by searching Weili's background and personality as revealed by her reactions to her experiences.

In the background of Weili's childhood insecurities flit brief snapshots of her mother—combing her hair, examining her face in the mirror, offering her daughter an English biscuit. There is no explicit reason for the mother's second-rate position in Jiang's life, but the lack of a son suggests that Jiang might have resented the birth of a girl. Independent, rebellious, the mother sets the norm for Weili by smiling while pouring out angry words to Jiang and by retreating into her lonely room, perhaps to nurture romantic daydreams of Lu. For Weili, the penalty for independence strikes when her mother can no longer pay the cost. It is Weili who must endure a blend of "funny and bad stories, terrible secrets and romantic tales" told about the runaway mother.

Significant is the fact that Weili later attends her mother's alma mater, the Catholic missionary school in Shanghai, and enjoys some degree of wealth and privilege as her mother's *syin ke*, or "little heart." This establishment of place in a household hierarchy of women precedes an unexpected adaptation to another household, where her aunts and cousins outnumber Uncle. In her pathetic attempts to make sense of her mother's disappearance, Weili gathers slivers of facts and raw shards of gossip along with needling from her uncle's family, who take no delight in another girlchild to raise. In sorrow after her mother leaves, Weili too willingly accepts guilt, admitting to Pearl: "In my heart, there is a little room. And in that room is a little girl, still six years old. She is always waiting, an achy hoping, hoping beyond reason." To fill that empty niche, Weili waters a dried flower bulb hoping "it would grow into a fairy maiden who could be my playmate."

In her optimistic moments, the adult Winnie is a natural wit—sometimes unintentionally so. Some of the novel's best lines owe their grace and charm to her refreshing candor: "How can I sing 'Silent Night, Joy to the World,' when I want to shout and say, So glad he is dead! Wrong thought, wrong day." On a minor pilgrimage about her home, she makes the womanly gestures that reveal her makeup—the bargains from Happy Super, a private moment to dust Jimmy's picture, an anticlimactic frown at a *Playboy* that Samuel bought in 1964. Perhaps intuitively, she fears that she will pass into the distant chambers of her family's heart like Auntie Du, who smelled of mothballs. Already, like Alice in Wonderland hoping that her cat Dinah misses her, Winnie feels unneeded, disconnected, and believes that no one listens to her since Jimmy died and left her to manage for herself.

Too introspective, too demanding of self and children, Winnie recalls the turbulent teen years when she warned Pearl against tampons, blue eye shadow, and attachment to "that Randy boy" who asked for a beer. Winnie's narrative follows the stages of coming to knowledge through three levels:

1. from *scapegoating* ("Confucius, that awful man who made that society")
2. to *appreciating and celebrating female strength*, illustrated by the woman with the broom searching for a child buried in rubble and crying, "My fault! My fault!"
3. and finally to *verbalizing* her first anger and defiance of Wen Fu.

After Danru's birth, Weili congratulates herself for changing gradually, for exploring her feelings, and for getting to know Gan, a friend and potential lover. The setbacks sting her vulnerable ego, reminding her "How foolish I was! To think my body was my own." Like Joan of Arc facing the societal and religious establishment of her time, Weili smiles at the courtroom and shouts, "I would rather sleep on the concrete floor of a jail . . . than go to that man's house." Only Winnie knows how much that brazen smile cost her.

Later in her life, Winnie climbs from the pit of patriarchal oppression by observing and by recovering from her own mistakes. She readily admits to Pearl that Samuel was second in her love. Concerning Hulan, she chafes at the very qualities that kept her alive during the war years: candor, spunk in delivering the unnamed villager's baby, and an effort to end the secrecy and lying that isolate Winnie from Pearl. Winnie stereotypes the young Hulan as plump, plain, and unfashionable like laundry hung out to dry, with backwoods manners. Unlike Weili, who grew up among genteel people, Hulan harbors no prudery about her body, relishes the imaginative superstition about a magic spring, and provides the red skirt that enables Old Mr. Ma to ease the truck over treacherous mountain passes to safety. Weili recognizes signs of weakness in Hulan that are correctable: she overeats during famine so she can avoid the hunger she recalls from her past, and she appreciates new glasses, through which she studies Chinese characters as Weili teaches her to read.

Through strengths and faults, Weili and Hulan profit from their wartime sisterhood when events drag them down. The parallel development of Weili and Hulan—choosing husbands who had been involved with other women, laboring to upgrade infested housing, and grieving for the deaths of Danru and Jiaguo after the epidemic—suggests that their lives are so intertwined that they share too many secrets, too many projects, too many sorrows that no one else can appreciate. In the end, Helen giggles to Pearl, "I said I was going to die so you would both tell each other your secrets." Like Little Yu's mother and Peanut, Helen has always respected Winnie's courage and has treasured the jade earrings that represent Winnie's tie with the most precious woman in her life, her mother.

Overall, Tan speaks the story of Weili with a kind of pride in womanly courage that comes from experience and from knowing Daisy Tan, a mother just like Winnie. As Tan notes in *The Moon Lady:*

> But you see, I had already found myself. I found out what kind of tiger I really was. Because I now knew there were many kinds of wishes, some that came from my stomach, some that were selfish, some that came from my heart. And I knew what the best wishes were: those I could make come true by myself.

In shaping her own destiny, Weili has the courage to defy and shoot at Wen Fu, toss his pants out the window, rejoice at his death, then burn him in effigy and enjoy his agonies in hell. Helen congratulates Winnie for, years ago, having swallowed water from the magic spring, the antidote to bitterness and "changing everything—your stomach, your heart, your mind. Everything sweet." Winnie, careful not to leave the last word to Helen, retorts, "Peaceful . . . no worries, no sorrows."

Selecting a personal goddess for the altar of the deposed Kitchen God, one which she will give to her daughter Pearl, is Winnie's ultimate act of self-determination.

## TAN'S LITERARY INGREDIENTS

In *The Kitchen God's Wife*, Amy Tan has so expertly combined many diverse literary elements that they become individually transparent to the reader, who becomes caught up in the events and the lives of its characters. The reader is a little like a hungry diner tasting for the first time the product of an elaborate recipe with a unique and haunting taste that cannot be traced to its many individual ingredients. Tan's "literary ingredients" include structural framework, point of view and voice; Chinese culture; Chinese history; humor; and figures of speech and other stylistic tools.

*Structural Framework, Point of View, and Voice.* Concerning the first category of ingredients, Tan's use of the **first-person singular voice** is hardly unique in literature, especially in the narration of personal experiences. However, Tan employs the first-person voice in unique ways that facilitate the **structural framework** of the novel: The heart of the novel (Chapters 5 through 24) is Winnie Louie's first person narration of her life story to her daughter, Pearl, including digressions and comments. This technique exemplifies the traditional literary form of *confession,* a self-told revelation of one's life and philosophy often intended as a psychological release from guilt and blame through introspection, explanation, and rationalization, blended with the narration of events. Winnie attempts to free herself of the burden of being an abandoned child, a battered wife during wartime, a mother terminating unwanted pregnancies through abortion, a jailed prisoner, and a runaway wife, hoping to convince Pearl that adult choices made under duress—often just trying to stay alive and preserve some spiritual and emotional wholeness—transcend morality. Winnie's confession, by virtue of its honesty and vigor, indicates that she is neither timid nor contrite in her efforts to gain Pearl's understanding and acceptance, as well as to put her own life into perspective from the vantage point of her age.

Winnie's **narrative** follows in a rich literary tradition; for example, consider the story told by Jane Pittman, a participant in the Louisiana civil rights movement and title character in Ernest Gaines' fictional *The Autobiography of Miss Jane Pittman,* and that of Jack Crabb, the bi-national spokesman and picaresque participant at the Battle of Little Big Horn in Thomas Berger's *Little Big Man.* Winnie speaks not only from her own experience, but often represents the ongoing experiences of others: pilots pitted against a superior enemy air force, wives doomed to wait and hope, refugees relying on shreds of rumor for their compass needle, and noncombatants who must choose an allegiance in chancy times. Winnie's voice accommodates views and ideas of her mother, Helen, Auntie Du, Min, Peanut, Jimmy Louie, even Wen Fu and other characters, but the **controlling vision** is always Winnie's.

This confession of Winnie's past is set within the framework of present-day events and concerns, still narrated in first person, but with a difference. One of the central issues of the novel is the emotional distance between Winnie and her daughter, Pearl, both of whom are entrenched in secrets that each of them withholds from the other. Tan shifts point of view between the two women to highlight this psychological separation: In the first two chapters, Pearl introduces the present-day circumstances, including her concern about the multiple sclerosis she hides from her mother. Pearl narrates this not only in first person, but in *present tense*, giving immediacy and urgency to the opening of the novel. Her first-person voice returns again immediately after her mother completes her confession (Chapter 25). In Chapters 3 and 4, Winnie leads up to her confession in first person, *past tense*, and returns to the same voice and tense in Chapter 26. Significantly, Winnie's final words of the novel, as if spoken to Pearl, are in *present tense*.

Remarkably the events which set in motion the story's structure are precipitated by neither of the two principals—Winnie or Pearl—but by a third party, Helen, Winnie's argumentative and opinionated **foil**. By manipulating her own secrets and threatening to "tell all" in the interest of clearing the air as part of the Chinese New Year tradition, Helen is the agent who brings Winnie and Pearl face to face in order for them to share secrets and bridge the emotional distance between them. Helen functions as a kind of insider **deus ex machina.**

*Chinese Culture.* Amy Tan's Chinese-American heritage bubbles to the surface so naturally that the reader gradually becomes suffused in Chinese lore, like the fragrance given off by the green tea leaves that cover the floor of the women's bathhouse in Hangchow while they wash and relax in hot water. Examples of Chinese culture that contribute substantially to the story include:

- the rituals and celebrations of the Chinese New Year
- accepted roles for women in society and in the family
- polygamy as a feudal custom
- dowry for a bride
- acceptability of concubines
- the manner of opening presents
- *yin/yang* energies

- curses, fates, good luck, bad luck
- fortune telling
- table-top altars to household gods
- Chinese zodiac and astrology
- Chinese numerology
- Buddhist ceremonies and related ideas, especially about death
- Chinese foods and eating customs

Tan's smooth integration of a particular culture into her storyline has many significant literary counterparts, even if we limit our view to regional, historical, and ethnic cultures within the United States—for example, Margaret Mitchell's *Gone with the Wind*, Toni Morrison's *Beloved*, Richard Wright's *Native Son*, John Steinbeck's *The Grapes of Wrath*, and any of Tony Hillerman's detective novels.

*Chinese History.* Just as Tan has immersed the reader in cultural lore, she has also plunged the reader into the maelstrom of modern Chinese history, not the most familiar locale or period of world history for American readers. Her storyline is woven tightly through the events of internal political infighting between Nationalists and Communists, as well as the center-stage imperialist actions of the Japanese. (Key events are listed in the earlier section of these Notes titled **Chronology of Historical and Fictional Events**.) Direct references as well as allusions are made to such significant elements in Chinese history as:

- the history of the Kuomintang, beginning in patriotism and valor and deteriorating over the years into corruption and brutality
- the history of communism in China, in much the reverse pattern—beginning haltingly and, amidst suppression and disdain, gradually growing into strength and dedicated leadership
- the power of the warlords during periods of weak central government
- the assistance and influence of the United States in China, including the unusual relationship between Claire Chennault and the Nationalist government, represented by Chiang Kai-shek

- the Nationalists' own accidental bombing of Shanghai, as well as later bombings by the Japanese of Shanghai, Nanking, Kunming, and many other cities
- the gradual encroachment of the Japanese territorial take-overs, requiring moves not only of the Chinese air bases, but also of the Nationalist seat of government
- the importance of the Burma Road, and the result of the British in closing it temporarily at a crucial time
- the Japanese occupation of Shanghai and their recruiting of collaborators
- the Nationalist abandonment of mainland China for a final stand on Formosa (Taiwan) as the Communists establish the People's Republic of China on the mainland.

The history Tan did *not* mention is as noteworthy as what she included. For example, Weili as a young Shanghai schoolgirl must have learned something of the Japanese encroachments in northern China that preceded the Chinese declaration of war against Japan in 1937. However, she may not have been aware of the parallel invasions of territory by the Germans in Europe that preceded the declaration of World War II in 1939. Weili makes no mention of the bombing of Pearl Harbor, which brought the U.S. into the war, or the use of the U.S. atom bomb to end the war, although she celebrates the defeat of the Japanese, without mentioning why they surrendered. The absence of information about such major foreign incidents in the stories of participants illustrates that, to those directly involved in their own survival, distant events do not seem significant and may not even be known.

Amy Tan's depiction of the effects of the Chinese-Japanese War on fictional characters belongs to a long and respected tradition of works written by authors who, without firsthand knowledge, intensify for the reader the realities of war by placing imaginary victims in the midst of real disasters of war. In this way, they create for the reader scenes which become immediate and tangible with dust, fear, shrieks of pain, and the smell of death. Fiction thus allows us to experience the stampede at Antietam, firebombs over Dresden, cries of the wounded whom Napoleon deserted on his flight from Moscow, and the rain of Patriot missiles during the Persian Gulf War. This tradition is further illustrated in such novels as *The Red Badge of Courage* (Stephen Crane), *The Persian Boy* (Mary

Renault), *Fallen Angels* (Walter Dean Myers), and *Gone with the Wind* (Margaret Mitchell).

Like these forerunners, Tan relies on research and secondhand descriptions to create fictitious firsthand accounts of fear and panic. In this novel, Weili/Winnie identifies this terrible mental state by the Chinese word *taonan*—the loss of logic, hope, and sanity preceding flight from looming destruction. In the life-threatening moment when thinking equates with self-preservation, Hulan makes choices like those that save Crane's Henry Fleming, Renault's Bagoas, Myers' green recruits in Vietnam, and Mitchell's Scarlett O'Hara. For Hulan, staying alive during the bombardment of Nanking means carrying a stout stick and clubbing anyone who threatens to steal her purloined pedicab, with which she rescues Winnie from trampling, or worse.

In the style of Randall Jarrell's poignant five-line poem "Death of the Ball Turret Gunner," Tan identifies with the false detachment experienced by the Kuomintang airman. She even manages to find a shred of hope for the barbarous Wen Fu, who luxuriates in clouds as his fighter plane mounts to the skies. In a somber mood, she visualizes how planes loaded with bombs violate all nature, including human life, by focusing on isolated limbs and debris in the wake of a Japanese bombing of the Kunming marketplace, and by describing the deathbed agony of Gan, Winnie's "ghost lover," who is disemboweled as a result of air combat.

Conrad Richter's novel *The Light in the Forest* depicts the homeless True Son, an innocent victim, reared by the Lenni Lenape, who suffers post-war trauma after being returned to a hostile family and community. Similar in its empathy, Tan's novel pictures Winnie as a septuagenarian quailing at the squawk of a smoke alarm as though her abusive husband had returned from the afterlife to degrade and torment her. As Jimmy Louie surmises, tenuous human relations that are fraught with shortages of food, fear of invasion, makeshift living arrangements, and separation from family are likely to snap under the strain of protracted war.

The success of such fictionalized war images derives from the author's ability to reduce thousands of maimed bodies, burned-out buildings, collapsed governmental structures, ruined dreams, and shattered relationships to a handful of realistic characters surrounded by glimpses of the walking wounded—the widowed Wan

Bettys, the poorly supplied Jiaguos, tattered evacuees from targeted cities, and unburied remains of noncombatants whose lives end during an accidental bombing of an unsuspecting city.

More powerful than statistical records, chronicles, histories, logbooks, film clips, and journalistic reportage, the fictional mode allows the reader to experience a miniaturized story of struggle that personalizes war. Ken Burns' recounting of the American Civil War, both in print and on video, provides comprehensive information and insights from numerous points of view; in contrast, by focusing on Winnie, Tan presents the reader an experience in a cruel war from the perpective of a single life.

*Humor.* Lest the reader be overwhelmed and horrified by unrelieved accounts of suffering or deprivation, Tan allows two of her main characters—Winnie and Helen—to survive many troublesome circumstances with humor, both intentional and unintentional. Winnie's humor is usually gentle, frequently subtle, sometimes unknowing. For example, Winnie comments about agreeing to an arranged marriage: "And suddenly someone came knocking at my door—and he was charming, a reason to dream about a better life. What else could I do? I let him in."

Winnie's telephone conversation with Pearl in Chapter 1 illustrates her accidental humor:

- Pearl learns from her mother about Auntie Du's death: "What was it?" Pearl asks. "A stroke?" Her mother answers, "A bus."
- Winnie (who co-owns a flower shop with Helen) says of Auntie Du, "She was a good lady. Fourteen wreaths already," adding in a whisper, "Of course, we are giving everyone twenty-percent discount."
- Pearl's husband Phil tries to tell Winnie that his family will stay in a motel when they visit. Winnie says, "Why waste money that way? You can stay at my house, plenty of rooms." Phil says, "No, no, really. It's too much trouble. Really." And Winnie replies, "Trouble for who?"

Helen's humorous comments or retorts often have a bite to them, more a reflection of her lack of education in manners than of any malice or criticism. Commenting on a newcomer to Jimmy's church, Helen says, "He's a doctor, but he only put a five-dollar bill in the offering tray."

When Winnie is critical of Helen's purchase of a fish that is not fresh, she asks Helen, "Ai, do you know what happens when fish are three days old?" Helen immediately replies, "They swim out to sea."

And when Helen refers to the new business of their mutual friend, Wan Betty, she makes an approving appraisal with: "A clothing shop. Ladies' things, all discount."

*Figures of Speech and Other Stylistic Tools.* A student of language both as reader and professional writer, Amy Tan demonstrates her own gift of integrating literary tools such as figures of speech and other stylistic tools so well that they become a natural part of her writing. Sprinkled throughout the narrative, her usages can dazzle the reader when the occasion calls for a skilled turn of phrase. Several examples are illustrated below.

**alliteration**
- Everyone in the family has been calling him Bao-bao ever since he was a baby, which is what *bao-bao* means, "precious baby."

- It is the altar for Grand Auntie's good-luck god, the Chinese crèche.

**allusion**
- . . . the way she could peel an apple all in one long curly piece so that it lay on my hand like a flat yellow snake.

- I had seen many moving pictures before with my mother, all silent: Charlie Chaplin, the fatty man, policemen and fire engines, the cowboys running their racehorses in a circle.

**aphorism**
- He who pats the horse's ass deserves the dung of a donkey.
- When the tree dies, the grass underneath withers.

**blandishment**
- She always called me *syin ke*, a nickname, two words that mean "heart liver," the part of the body that looks like a tiny heart.
- But when she turned around, she held out her hand to me and said, *"Tang jie"*—sugar sister, the friendly name we sometimes used for one another when we were younger.

**dialect and idiom**
- "Hey, Phil, bro'," Bao-bao calls, pouring more champagne.
- And later I heard that "cat's ears" was only a local expression for wonton soup.

**euphemism**
- When servants tell you there's a ghost, it means something is wrong and they are not in the position to tell you why.
- These girls were called "roadside wives," and every few steps, it seemed, I passed one standing in front of a three-stool restaurant, or a wine shop only as wide as a door, or a steep stairway leading to a second-story teahouse.

**foreshadowing**
- Of course, the next morning we heard what really happened.
- I could not make just one choice, I had to make two: Let me live. Let my father die.

**housewifely lore**
- The cloth holding all this in was thin, had never had hot water poured over it to tighten the threads.
- Steamed fish doesn't taste good the next day.

**humor**
- He is not Santa Claus. More like a spy—FBI agent, CIA, Mafia, worse than IRS, that kind of person!
- She pulled out an orange and put that on the table, then two bags of airline peanuts, restaurant toothpicks, her extra wallet for tricking robbers. She turned the purse sideways and spilled out all sorts of other junk in case a war breaks out and we have to run away like the old days: two short candles, her American naturalization papers in a plastic pouch, her Chinese passport from forty years ago, one small motel soap, one washcloth, one pair each of knee-high stockings and nylon panties, still brand-new.

**imagery**
- The tail of the dragon was nudging Peanut, and he turned out to be Wen Fu.
- Just like a dragon whose tail had been stepped on. She did not know how to hide her feelings the way I did.

**local color**
- This was the mock play the village people put on every year on the last day, the same old tradition.
- She was the senior wife, the one who approved the spending of household money.

**metaphor**
- She said that a woman-body built its own nest once a month.
- Now that I remember it, that was when our friendship took on four splits and five cracks.

**onomatopoeia**
- The old revolutionaries, the new revolutionaries, the Kuomintang and the Communists, the warlords, the bandits, and the students— gwah! gwah! gwah!—everybody squabbling, like old roosters claiming the same sunrise.
- It was a rare little fish, called *wah-wah yu*, because it cried just like a baby—wah-wah!—and it could wave its arms and legs.

**parallelism**
- I was not worried, because I could feel it swimming inside of me, turning its body around, pushing with its feet, rolling its head.
- She was tearing it away—my protective shell, my anger, my deepest fears, my despair.

**puns**
- It was his bad heart that kept him alive! And now I was the one left with a bad heart.

**repetition**
- Two? Only two people wanted that job?
- Each time hope failed for someone else, I made a promise, promise after promise.

**simile**
- I watched my daughter open her mouth wide like a baby bird, and my mother dropped the morsel in.
- Unfortunately Helen's mind wanders everywhere, like a cow following grass wherever its mouth goes.

## SETTINGS

One of Tan's "literary ingredients"—the settings in which the action of *The Kitchen God's Wife* takes place—deserves separate analysis because the settings play such a significant role in this book. They are not mere pictorial background for the scenes, but virtually characters in their own right.

China—especially the China of the war years—is not a familiar locale to most Western readers. Choosing to tell a story in such an environment risks confusing the reader with unfamiliar sights, sounds, and situations, if not so distancing the reader that he or she puts the book down forever. Tan is especially successful in minimizing both of these possibilities. The reader is instead compelled to continue the story for its own sake while gradually experiencing more and more comfort and compatibility with the foreign settings.

Tan eases into unfamiliar settings by beginning the story in California with a familiar situation—an American couple (Pearl and Phil) experiences tension over the demands of the wife's mother (Winnie). Even the engagement banquet scene in Chinatown is one most readers can identify with—encountering family members one would rather not spend time with, observing the petty jealousies and jibes of one relative toward another, enduring solicitous comments and questions of those not really interested. Pearl's visit to her mother's flower shop in Chinatown gently introduces the reader to several details of Chinese culture, and later the Buddhist funeral plunges Pearl—and the reader—into a much more alien environment. Tan backs off from the foreign setting briefly while Winnie fussily cleans her house in preparation for telling the long story that follows, so the reader is reassured that Winnie is at least currently a rather ordinary American widow living alone in the home where her family was raised.

As Winnie tells her life story to Pearl, a woman with little connection to her Chinese heritage, she has to explain details of the Chinese settings and customs to Pearl—and thus to the reader. And so we are all—Pearl and readers together—quickly swept up into the exotic setting in pre-war Shanghai.

Notable uses of setting, both as passive scenery and as active contributors to plot and mood, are the following:

**Weili's Shanghai home and Shanghai itself.** The elegance of the home and the wealth and status of the family are clearly established, along with the wonders of 1925 Shanghai and the strangeness of a feudal household containing several wives. The reader accompanies Weili and her mother on their last-day excursion of the sights and sounds of the city. Twelve years later (1937), the reader accompanies Weili and San Ma on a seven-day buying expedition for Weili's dowry. These visits contrast with several views of the city and the house in 1945 after the end of the war, when Weili, Wen Fu, and Danru return to Shanghai. The emotions of Weili and other characters are reflected here in their settings.

**Tsungming Island.** The house and town of Mouth of the River provide an early contrast with Shanghai, clearly illustrating Uncle's status as lower than Weili's father, but higher than other residents on the island. The New Year festival scene contributes a familiar country fair kind of atmosphere to the less familiar rituals of a traditional Chinese celebration. Weili's post-war visit to Tsungming Island and her foster home physically dramatizes the difficulties of survival and deprivation.

**Living quarters and surroundings at air bases.** The unfamiliar, primitive, and uncomfortable conditions of Weili and Wen Fu's quarters in the old monastery at Hangchow provide a harsh, ironic setting for Weili's early experiences with Wen Fu's crude sexual demands. In contrast, the surrounding beauty of the area, the special bathhouse she helps the women create, the walks with Hulan to the "magic spring" or the restaurant with noodle soup—all these physical and sensory experiences tend to ameliorate the humiliations of her new marriage.

Each of the subsequent air base settings—Yangchow, Nanking, and Kunming—has features that reflect Weili's gradual learning to cope with her circumstances, although never completely until she is back again in post-war Shanghai.

**The trips to and from Kunming.** The 1400-mile trip by boat and truck from Nanking to Kunming is a wonder of both explicit and implicit descriptions, climaxing at the top of the mountains near Heaven's Breath, before its descent into the dirt and crowding of Kunming. Again for contrast, the return trip in 1945 allows glimpses of the ravages on both people and the nation by the disasters of the war.

**Experiences in air raids.** The peaceful description of the Nanking marketplace and its colorful and delectable wares is torn apart by the strange air raid of propaganda leaflets, resulting in Weili's first experience of *taonan* and mass hysteria. By contrast, Weili's subsequent experiences in the bombing of Kunming become almost routine, except for her initial encounters with the horrors of violent death and mental aberration.

**Prison.** One would expect, especially from Weili's initial experience in jail before her trial, that her prison experience would be one of the lowest periods of her life—which has been filled with lows. Yet the primitive setting of the prison almost disappears in the soft light of her acceptance of her circumstances—having made a clear choice against Wen Fu—and in the warmth created by her reaching out to the women sharing her circumstance. We experience the surprise of anticipating a potentially disastrous situation and delighting instead in the glowing accomplishment for Weili—a kind of "final examination" of her adaptability and self-development.

Amy Tan's remarkable use of her settings—as foreign as many of them are—leaves the reader feeling that he or she has in a small way traveled with Weili through the diverse locales of an unfamiliar country, finding much to appreciate and to associate with other fragments of almost forgotten information about the country, its social history, and its people.

## THE ASIAN-AMERICAN LITERARY PHENOMENON

Tan's novels have become an instant *cause célèbre* in multicultural and women's studies, drawing attention to Asian Americans, a racial group often neglected in popular fiction until the success of works such as

Maxine Hong Kingston's *The Woman Warrior* and *Tripmaster Monkey*
Yoko Kawashima Watkins' *So Far from the Bamboo Grove*
Jeanne Wakatsuki Houston & James Houston's *Farewell to Manzanar*
Laurence Yep's *Dragonwings*, and
David Wong Louie's *Pang of Love*.

Among newer Asian-American colleagues, Tan's personal favorites include:

Belle Yang's *Baba: Odyssey of a Manchurian*
Ben Fong Torres' *The Rice Room*
Beth Yahp's *Crocodile Fury*
Jessica Hagedorn's *Dogeaters*
Gish Jen's *Typical American*, and
Gus Lee's *Honor and Duty*.

Tan accounts for this burst of first-generation American writers by claiming that improved English language skills give voice to the stories that actually belong to immigrant parents like John and Daisy

Tan. Book buyers and booksellers alike seem eager to prove Tan correct in assuming that this generation's stories are worth reading.

# REVIEW QUESTIONS AND ESSAY TOPICS

(1). Discuss how the legend of the Kitchen God and Auntie Du's table altar relate to the overall structure and story of *The Kitchen God's Wife*, both at a literal and a symbolic level. Why do you think Tan used the legend as the nominal theme? Illustrate with examples.

(2). Amy Tan opens the novel with the engagement banquet of a couple who seem to have little chance of lasting happiness and ends it with their wedding banquet. Why do you think she chose those events as part of the present-day framework for Winnie's story of her past? For your discussion, consider the betrothal of Weili to Wen Fu. Are there any signs in that engagement that the marriage might not be successful?

(3). Discuss the kinds of actions and activities that help the female characters of the novel endure privations, terror, loss, and loneliness during the war with Japan. Consider especially Weili, Hulan, Auntie Du, and Peanut. You may also draw upon characters such as Min, San Ma, Wan Betty, Little Yu's mother, New Aunt, Old Aunt, and women prisoners in the Shanghai prison.

(4). Using *The Kitchen God's Wife* as a source of ideas and examples, develop extended definitions of the following: feminism, feminist sisterhood, misogyny, repression, feudal marriage, and family.

(5). Using this novel as a model and resource, define, contrast, and illustrate the following literary concepts and devices: historical fiction, saga, legend, framework, oral tradition, protagonist/antagonist, literary foils, irony, satire, and denouement.

(6). Analyze the stratification of women in the traditional Chinese community, as presented in *The Kitchen God's Wife*. Using examples from the novel, show how positions such as the following differ from one another in society and in families: head wife, second wife, foster mother, concubine, servant, daughter, bride-to-be, bride, mother-in-law, illegitimate child, and entertainer.

(7). Describe the support system that enables Weili to endure arrest, trial, public humiliation, media slander, and imprisonment. Also discuss how this period of Weili's life illustrates her progress in taking control over her life in contrast with the early years of her marriage.

(8). Analyze the complex relationship between Weili/Winnie and Hulan/Helen from its beginning, through the war years, and into the present time. Why has the friendship continued, and even flourished, when the two women seem to be at odds so much of the time? Use examples from the novel.

(9). Discuss the contributions to the elucidation and movement of the story provided by the following minor characters: San Ma, Min, Wan Betty, Old Mr. Ma, Mochou, Tessa and Cleo, Gan, and Little Yu's mother.

(10). Compare Tan's portrayals of male characters in the novel—for example, Wen Fu, Jimmy Louie, Jiang Sao-yen, Jiaguo, Phil Brandt, Roger Kwong—with her portrayals of female characters. Illustrate with examples from the book.

(11). Develop a personality profile of Wen Fu, illustrating his primary traits and motivations with examples from the novel. Include a discussion of how Wen Fu's manipulative behavior leaves him open to crafty plots by others such as Weili, Hulan, Jiang Sao-yen, and Auntie Du. Consider the symbolic significance of when and how he died (at Christmas of heart disease).

(12). Analyze the conflicts between examples of these pairs of characters from the novel: wife/husband, mother/daughter, bride/mother-in-law, master/servant, officer/subordinate, and pairs of lovers, siblings, and business partners.

(13). Discuss the role in the novel of seemingly incidental events or items such as these: Auntie Du's funeral banner, the Hangchow bathhouse, the Nanking pedicab, Hulan's red skirt, Weili's broken heel, the imperial green jade earrings, mah jong, the box of donkey dung, the wall scroll panels in Jiang's house, ten pairs of silver chopsticks, and airplane tickets.

(14). Compose a woman's-eye view of World War II in contrast to the objective reporting of a history book, battlefield journal, or encyclopedia. Discuss the scenes of disorder and uncertainty as seen by women in transit from war zones to safety. Explain the hazards that women in flight contend with—for example, the threat of disease or injury, bad roads, inadequate news of the war effort, impure water supply, limited housing, primitive methods of transportation, infestations of vermin, famine, rationing, cold and exposure to the elements, faltering leadership, hostile insurgents, political upheaval, helplessness, divided loyalties, and inaccessible escape routes.

(15). In an article in *Glamour*, Amy Tan comments that she is aware of the "danger of being cast as a spokesperson." Why might it be difficult for Tan to publish books, stories, and essays featuring feminism, mother/daughter relations, war brides, immigrants, the American Dream, and first-generation Asian Americans without being considered an apologist?

(16). Analyze the Communist method of teaching Lu "One Thousand Characters in Ten Days" and Sequoyah's efficient syllabary and literacy program for the Cherokee nation. Explain why a similar program is not possible for the English language.

(17). Compare the use of the New Year motif in George Eliot's *Silas Marner* and Tan's *The Kitchen God's Wife*. How do Godfrey Cass, Nancy Lammeter, Eppie, and Silas reflect a new beginning similar to the change that alters the mother-daughter relationship in the Louie family? Contrast customs in Raveloe and Lantern Yard with those of Shanghai, Kunming, Tsungming Island, and San Francisco's Chinatown.

(18). Relate the destructive familial patterns in *The Kitchen God's Wife* to similar negative motifs in the Old Testament book of Genesis and in Tsao Hsueh-chin's *Dream of the Red Chamber*. Mention, for example, coercion, violence, duplicity, tyranny, apathy, selfishness, martyrdom, and patriarchy. Consider Shere Hite's opinions on the lives of women whom, she says, society, religion, and government relegate to subservient roles.

(19). Compare Amy Tan's descriptions of the changes that uproot Chinese traditions and power structure with similar alterations in books such as Pearl Buck's *The Good Earth*, Esther Hautzig's *The Endless Steppe*, N. Scott Momaday's *The Way to Rainy Mountain*, Zlata Filipovich's *Zlata's Diary*, Margaret Mitchell's *Gone with the Wind*, Theodora Kroeber's *Ishi*, Elie Wiesel's *Night*, Jessamyn West's *Except for Me and Thee*, and Chinua Achebe's *Things Fall Apart*.

(20). Compare the immigration/first-generation American motifs of *The Kitchen God's Wife* and *The Joy Luck Club* with similar situations in books such as Jeanne and James Houston's *Farewell to Manzanar*, Rudolfo Anaya's *Bless Me, Ultima*, Upton Sinclair's *The Jungle*, Gish Jen's *Typical American*, Laura Esquivel's *Like Water for Chocolate*, Sandra Cisneros' *The House on Mango Street*, and Henry Roth's *Call It Sleep*.

(21). Compare coping skills of strong female characters, especially Auntie Du, Winnie, and Helen in *The Kitchen God's Wife* with characters such as Scarlett O'Hara in Margaret Mitchell's *Gone with the Wind*, Sethe in Toni Morrison's *Beloved*, Olivia Rivers in Ruth Prawar Jhabvala's *Heat and Dust*, Celie and Sofia in Alice Walker's *The Color Purple*, Janie in Zora Neale Hurston's *Their Eyes Were Watching God*, Yoko and Ko in Yoko Kawashima Watkins' *So Far from the Bamboo Grove*, Sophie in William Styron's *Sophie's Choice*, and Sheba in Maya Angelou's poem *Now Sheba Sings the Song*. Extend this exercise to consider female protagonists in such films as *Daughters of the Dust*, *The Piano*, *Fried Green Tomatoes*, *Steel Magnolias*, *Playing for Time*, *Julia*, *Shadowlands*, and *Places in the Heart*.

# AMY TAN'S PUBLISHED WORKS

Novels
>    *The Joy Luck Club* (1989)
>    *The Kitchen God's Wife* (1991)
>    *The Hundred Secret Senses* (1995)

Anthologized Short Works
>    *State of the Language* (University of California Press, 1989)
>    *Best American Essays, 1991* (Ticknor & Fields, 1991)

Children's Fiction
>    *The Moon Lady* (1992)
>    *The Chinese Siamese Cat* (1994)

Individual Essays
>    "Mother Tongue," *Threepenny Review*. Fall 1990.
>    "Angst and the Second Novel," *Publishers Weekly*. April 5, 1991, 4-7.
>    "Lost Lives of Women," *Life*. April 1991, 90-91.
>    "Watching China," *Glamour*. September 1989, 302-303.

Individual Short Stories
>    "Endgame," *FM*. 1986.
>    "Fish Cheeks," *Seventeen*. December 1987, 99.
>    "Rules of the Game," *Seventeen*. November 1986, 106-108.
>    "Two Kinds," *Atlantic*. February 1989, 53-57.

# SELECTED BIBLIOGRAPHY

"Amy Tan" (interview), Phoenix *Arizona Republic*. October 5, 1993, n. p.

BAKER, JOHN F., "Fresh Voices, New Audiences," *Publishers Weekly*. August 9, 1993, 32-34.

BANNISTER, LINDA, "Three Women Revise: What Morrison, Oates, and Tan Can Teach Our Students about Revision," paper delivered to the Conference on College Composition and Communication. March 31-April 3, 1993, ERIC.

BARD, NANCY, "Adult Books for Young Adults," *School Library Journal*. December 1991, 149.

BERNIKOW, LOUISE, "Book Review," *Cosmopolitan*. June 1991, 36.

CHAMBERS, VERNICA, "Surprised by Joy," *Premiere*. October 1993, 80–84.

CHATFIELD-TAYLOR, JOAN, "*Cosmo* Talks to Amy Tan: Dazzling New Literary Light," *Cosmopolitan*. November 1989, 178.

CHUA, C. L., "Review," *Magill's Literary Annual*. Englewood Cliffs, N. J.: Salem Press, 1992.

CONDINI, NED, "Saints, Histories, Carnal Acts: Best Reads in 1991," *National Catholic Reporter*. November 22, 1991, 36.

*Contemporary Authors*. Vol. 136. Detroit: Gale Research, 1993.

DAVIS, EMORY, "An Interview with Amy Tan: Fiction—The Beast That Roams," *Writing-on-the-Edge*. Spring 1990, 97-111.

DEW, ROBB FORMAN, "Pangs of an Abandoned Child," *The New York Times Book Review*. June 16, 1991, sec 7, p. 9, col. 1.

DIXLER, ELSA, "Our Holiday Lists," *Nation*. December 30, 1991, 851–852.

DURRANT, SABINE, "Review," *London Times*. July 11, 1991, 16.

ERDRICH, LOUISE, "What Writers Are Reading," *Ms.* July/August 1991, 82–83.

FELDMAN, GAYLE, "Spring's Five Fictional Encounters of the Chinese American Kind," *Publishers Weekly*. February 8, 1991, 25–27.

"A Fiery Mother-Daughter Relationship," *USA Today*. October 5, 1993, D12.

FISHER, ANN H., "Fiction Review," *Library Journal*. June 1, 1991, 198.

FORAN, CHARLES, "Review," (Toronto) *Globe and Mail*. June 29, 1991. n. p.

GILLESPIE, ELZY, "Review," *San Francisco Review of Books*. Summer 1991, 33.

HUGHES, KATHRYN, "Sweet-Sour," *New Statesman and Society*. July 12, 1991, 37–38.

HUNT, ADAM PAUL, "Audio Reviews," *Library Journal*. July 1991, 154.

IYER, PICO, "The Second Triumph of Amy Tan," *Time*. June 3, 1991, 67.

KOENIG, RHODA, "Nanking Pluck," *New York*. June 17, 1991, 83–84.

"Lady Luck," Richmond (Virginia) *Times-Dispatch*. September 26, 1993, n. p.

LAW-YONE, WENDY, "Review," *Washington Post Book World*. June 16, 1991, 1–2.

LUCEY, ROSE MARCIANO, "Favorite New and Old Books of Certain Avid NCR Readers," *National Catholic Reporter*. November 19, 1993, 33.

MASLIN, JANET, "Intimate Generational Lessons, Available to All," *New York Times*. September 8, 1993, C15.

MATHEWS, LAURA, "More 'Joy Luck,'" *Glamour*. June 1991, 106.

MERINA, ANITA, "Joy, Luck, and Literature: Meet Amy Tan," *NEA Today*. October 1991, 9.

NEEDHAM, NANCY R., "By Their First Lines You Shall Know Them," *NEA Today*. May 1993, 27.

NELSON, SARA, "Picks and Pans," *People Weekly*. July 22, 1991, 21–22.

ONG, CAROLINE, "Re-writing the Old Wives' Tales," *Times Literary Supplement*. July 5, 1991, 20.

PETER, NELSON, and PETER FREUNDLICH, "Women We Love: Nine Women Who Knock Us Out," *Esquire*. August 1989, 86.

ROWLAND, PENELOPE, "American Woman," *Mother Jones*. July/August 1989, 10.

ROZAKIS, LAURIE NEU. *Cliffs Notes on* The Joy Luck Club. Lincoln, Neb.: Cliffs Notes, 1994.

SCHWARTZ, GIL, " . . . and Women of the Dunes," *Fortune*. August 26, 1991, 116.

SEAMAN, DONNA, "Quick Bibs," *American Libraries*. July 1991, 688.

SHAPIRO, LAURA, "From China, with Love," *Newsweek*. June 24, 1991, 63–64.

SOMOGYI, BARBARA, and DAVID STANTON, "Interview," *Poets & Writers Magazine*. September–October 1991, 24.

STEINBERG, SYBIL, "Fiction Review," *Publishers Weekly*. April 12, 1991, 45.

"Tan, Amy." *Current Biography*. Vol. 53, February 1992, 55.

TAN, AMY, "Excerpt of 'Kitchen God's Wife'," *McCall's*. July 1991, 115.

TAYLOR, NOEL, "The Luck of Amy Tan," *The Ottawa Citizen*. October 1, 1993, F1.

WOO, ELAINE, "Interview," *Los Angeles Times*. April 17, 1989, n. p.

YOUNG, PAMELA, "Mother with a Past: The Family Album Inspires a Gifted Writer," *Maclean's*. July 15, 1991, 47.

ZIA, HELEN, "A Chinese Banquet of Secrets," *Ms.* November/December 1991, 76–77.

ZINSSER, JOHN, "Audio Reviews—The Kitchen God's Wife Written and Read by Amy Tan," *Publishers Weekly.* June 7, 1991, 44.

# HISTORICAL BACKGROUND BIBLIOGRAPHY

ANSCHEL, EUGENE HOMER LEA. *Sun Yat-sen and the Chinese Revolution.* Westport, Ct.: Greenwood, 1984.

ARCHER, JULES. *Mao Tse-Tung.* New York: Hawthorn Books, 1972, 89.

BROWNSTONE, DAVID M. *The Chinese-American Heritage.* New York: Facts on File, 1988.

"Chiang Ch'ing," *Current Biography.* New York: H. W. Wilson, 1975.

EASTMAN, LLOYD, ET AL. *The Nationalist Era in China, 1927–1949.* New York: Cambridge University Press, 1991.

SCOTT, ROBERT L., JR. *God Is My Co-Pilot.* Reynoldsburg, Ohio: Buckeye Aviation Books, 1988.

STANLEY, ROY M. *Prelude to Pearl Harbor: War in China, 1937–41—Japan's Rehearsal for World War II.* New York: Scribners, 1982.

TERRELL, ROSS. *The White-Boned Demon: A Biography of Madame Mao Zedong.* New York: Morrow, 1984.

WITKE, ROXANE. *Comrade Chiang Ch'ing.* Boston: Little, Brown, 1977.

# NOTES

# NOTES

# NOTES

# NOTES